Reviews for *The 7-Day GL Diet*

'The (7-Day) GL diet, combined with exercise,
is one of the best around.'
Review of 3 diets, Radio 1 Newsbeat,
19 January 2006

THE CAN'T FAIL 7-DAY DIET.
'Yes, it's a brilliant, no-panic party-dress diet but
it's so much more besides. It'll teach you how to
stick cravings right where they belong – out of your life!'
Zest, **January 2006 issue**

'The Crash Diet that's Healthy and WORKS!'
Elle, **January 2006 issue**

'Only The 7-Day GL Diet proved to be an affordable option –
incorporating healthy foods that aren't overly expensive.'
Celebrity Diet Now, **Winter 2006**
**(article comparing the cost of buying the
food you need to follow the popular diets)**

'The GI has long been popular with celebs such as
Kim Cattrall and Jodie Kidd – now they can follow
a new improved version – the GL Diet.'
'If you're determined to start 2006 with an improved diet,
they don't get more user friendly than this one.'
Now, **29 December 2005**

Reviews for *The GL Diet*

'Try the easy new GL Diet – everyone's talking about it!'
***Essentials* (UK), June 2005**

'Choice is back on the menu.'
***The Times*, 14 May 2005**

'An easy weight loss plan for life … simpler than
GI and makes better sense …'
***Evening Standard*, 4 January 2005**

'… the GI diet has been superseded by a more
sophisticated version: the glycaemic load (GL) …'
***The Times*, 14 May 2005**

'The GI diet is so last year. Take slimming one stage further with GL,
a more sophisticated way of measuring the impact of food on your
body's energy levels. Now you can love your lunch but still
lose those love handles.'
***The Times*, 7 May 2005**

'The Glycaemic Load (GL) is the final part of the jigsaw.
Testing for the GI (glycaemic index) of foods is a fantastic
breakthrough, but it only gives half the true picture.'
***Essentials* (South Africa), September 2005**

'A good guide is Nigel Denby's *The GL Diet* … more useful …
more of a way of eating than a diet book.'
***handbag.com*, April 2005**

'Denby's writing is refreshingly clear and easy to understand; there's no high-tech scientific waffle … it's a simple programme that uses a food selection system based on science, on fact not fad, but most importantly it's been designed to be practical and easy to follow.'

Seven Magazine, *Sunday Mail* **(Cyprus), 3 April 2005**

'The GL diet has been instrumental in helping me get back to my pre-pregnancy weight. It's more than a diet though and has just become a way of life. I've got so much energy and don't have any of those food cravings I'd always associated with diets and healthy eating – I love it!'

Mishal Husain, news anchor,
BBC World News **and** *BBC News 24*

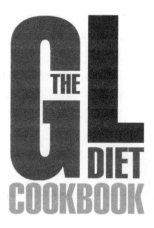

THE GL DIET COOKBOOK

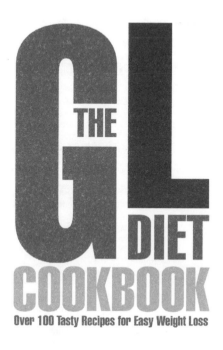

THE GL DIET COOKBOOK

Over 100 Tasty Recipes for Easy Weight Loss

Nigel Denby

with Tina Michelucci & Deborah Pyner

HarperThorsons
An Imprint of HarperCollins*Publishers*
77–85 Fulham Palace Road,
Hammersmith, London W6 8JB

The website address is: www.thorsonselement.com

and *HarperThorsons* are trademarks of
HarperCollins*Publishers* Ltd

First published by HarperThorsons 2006

1 3 5 7 9 10 8 6 4 2

A catalogue record of this book is
available from the British Library

ISBN-13 978-0-00-722576-7
ISBN-10 0-00-722576-8

Printed and bound in Great Britain by
Clays Ltd, St Ives plc

Contents

Acknowledgements

Thanks to Susanna, Laura, Chris and Sarah at HarperCollins for all your hard work, encouragement and support.

A huge thank you also to our ever-increasing band of Diet Freedom supporters, gathered from our previous books, *The 7-Day GL Diet* and *The GL Diet*, our website www.dietfreedom.co.uk and by word of mouth. It is your support that continues to motivate us to do better, and help you to the best of our ability in achieving your goals. Your honesty and feedback are invaluable and much admired.

Last but not least, not forgetting our wonderful partners, families and friends who have been unwavering in their support of our working hours and our passion in getting things right, even when we are painful to live with!

Thank you so much.

Lots of love,

Tina, Deborah and Nigel
xxx

Introduction

There is little doubt that in recent years the principles of low-glycaemic eating have gathered more and more support from dieticians, doctors and health organizations such as Diabetes UK and leading heart health and cancer charities.

The concept of being able to determine a food's effect on blood sugars has been described as 'the most significant nutritional development for 50 years' and has been conclusively shown to be a solution to a lifetime of yo-yo dieting for millions of people.

Unlike so many other weight-loss plans, the low-glycaemic approach is well respected as not only an effective weight-control tool but also for a host of health benefits, including reduced risk of heart disease, diabetes, high blood pressure and some cancers.

The Glycaemic Index (GI), which is the basis of low-glycaemic diets, is not a new idea. It has been researched and developed at major universities around the world for the past 25 years, but only really hit the mainstream a few years ago.

As with all science, nutrition is constantly evolving. What started as a complicated (and in some cases inaccurate) way of classifying carbohydrate-containing foods, the Glycaemic Index (GI), has been developed into a simpler, more accurate, user-friendly system in the Glycaemic Load (GL).

The Glycaemic Index classifies some foods we know to be inherently 'healthy' as being foods we should avoid. It also suggests other foods can be eaten freely, when in fact they may have a detrimental effect on our all-important blood sugars – why the inconsistency?

Simple – the Glycaemic Index is a laboratory test which requires that *specific amounts* of different foods are tested in order to produce comparable results. The Glycaemic Index doesn't take into account the amount of food we actually eat, and so the Index on its own can be misleading and confusing.

The Glycaemic Load removes these confusions and inaccuracies. It means more food choices and less room for error.

Having used the GL principles with my patients for some years now in my clinics, what I can tell you is that using the GL is the most effective weight-loss tool I have seen in my career, and the results achieved and feedback from our Diet Freedom Club Members online at www.diet-freedom.co.uk has reinforced this tenfold.

My patients, our readers and our Diet Freedom Club Members get results, maintain them, and tell us that for the first time in years they feel free of the 'diet trap' and able to get on with their lives. They feel well, have more energy and rediscover a long-lost optimistic outlook on life – something they have been missing for years. What more could we ask of an eating plan?

The principle of the GL diet is simple: Stable blood sugars means less excess energy stored as fat and fewer food cravings. We have been very careful in our previous books (*The GL Diet* and *The 7-Day GL Diet*), as in this cookbook, to ensure that our recipes and advice tick *all* the healthy eating boxes.

As well as eating low-GL foods, we advocate good fats, no added salt wherever possible, plenty of fruit and vegetables and good-quality proteins including fish, lean meats and poultry, pulses and, of course, a good dose of physical activity – not 'exercise' – we don't like that word – no, it's got to be **A C T I V I T Y** and it's got to be fun!

This isn't a here-today, gone-tomorrow fad diet. I wouldn't put my name to it if it were. This is a way of eating you can adopt for life, and it is very satisfying to see that more and more people are finding it offers them what no other diet has before: results and, more importantly, results they can maintain for ever.

What we've done with this cookbook is make an already simple principle even easier. You don't have to do any boring counting (who has the time?!) or weighing of foods (unless you want to), and there is absolutely no need to be hungry – so don't worry, you won't be.

So what a low-GL diet DOES mean is delicious food you'll love, food that loves you back, and heaps of variety to make sure you get all the nutritional goodies you need.

It also means 'time freedom'. If you are as busy as most of us, you probably won't want to come home after a tiring day and start preparing a whole host of weird and wonderful ingredients before you can even start cooking! Tina and Deborah have made sure that they have included lots of quick and easy recipes with this in mind.

We've designed a simple low-GL template for your guidance so that you can slot in whatever recipes you fancy. Choose from our 'fast and friendly' selection for quick, throw-together no-nonsense cooking, or from the host of veggie-friendly recipes. Our vegetarian friends are so often forgotten when it comes to diets, so we've taken some interesting ingredients to give you anything but the normal humdrum veggie selection.

And then, for when you have the time and inclination and feel like pushing the boat out a bit, we've got some delicious foodie-friendly recipes for keen cooks. Maybe you fancy a lazy breakfast and have a bit more time to prepare it, or you have friends or family over for dinner? We at Diet Freedom HQ love food and get a real buzz out of preparing good food for the people we love, so we hope you'll find the foodie-friendly recipes great for those special occasions.

Bon appetit!

Nigel Denby
Registered Dietician
RD BSc Hons

Chapter 1

HOW TO USE THIS BOOK

First and foremost we want you to enjoy this cookbook.

The last thing we want is for you to get hung up about working out or counting up the GL scores of foods, or weighing out every ingredient, so don't do any of that. Counting is boring and stressful and can lead to overeating in itself.

The basis of all the recipes is that we have swapped high-GL ingredients for low-GL ones. So if the recipe contains carbs, we have replaced the FAST carbs with SLOW ones.

We've also put together all the other pieces of the 'healthy eating jigsaw' to make sure that your low-GL diet is nicely balanced and full of lots of good, healthy and nutritious foods.

Rather than giving you very prescriptive plans and menus ('you must eat this today for breakfast and that for lunch tomorrow'), we've given you a basic template to help you plan your own low-GL healthy eating a week at a time. The template will help you make sure you eat regularly, eat a good variety of foods and, of course, choose the foods you love.

Now, because we've done everything we can think of to make using this cookbook as easy as possible, we want you to do something for us. We want you to 'think natural' and try, wherever possible, to start with basic ingredients, follow a few simple steps and end up with a delicious, natural, healthy dish. We're talking about cooking from scratch, not fancy *cordon bleu* stuff, just simple 'back to basics' cooking.

We are passionate about cutting back on highly processed foods because they can be full of hidden sugars, salt, additives and unhealthy trans fats. The bottom line with all of our recipes is that you start with a bunch of natural ingredients and combine them together. This means you are in total control over what you consume, with no hidden 'nasties' to worry about. We have also given you lots of short-cuts to help save you time and effort, without compromising on any of the health and taste benefits.

Weight Loss and A Whole Lot More

Low GL is about a lot more than weight loss. That's why more and more national and international health organizations are joining together to recommend a low-GL diet as the most appropriate for good health. Diabetes, high blood pressure, heart disease, some cancers and the symptoms of hormonal disturbances like Polycystic Ovarian Syndrome (PCOS), premenstrual syndrome (PMS) and the menopause can all be prevented or eased by a low-GL diet.

Let's Get Down to Basics

OK, so now we know why following a low-GL diet is so good for weight control and general health, let's get on with it! The basic templates (pages 15 and 19) will help you with balanced menu planning and shopping. We've based the templates on the basic principles of a healthy, balanced diet.

For instance, most of us know we should eat some oily fish every week, have five portions of fruit and veg every day and include dairy foods, which are a good source of calcium for healthy bones. The templates show you how to organize healthy low-GL eating by thinking about your day, deciding how much time you've got to prepare food, whether you'll be eating on the run or eating out, and balancing your foods throughout the day. If you have meat for lunch, you probably don't need meat again for dinner. Or if you struggle to eat a substantial breakfast, make sure you have a decent mid-morning snack to help you stay in the driving seat till lunch time.

The templates will give you the confidence to know that you are not only lowering your overall glycaemic load (GL) but also eating a good balance of food and nutrients at the same time.

The Principles of Healthy Eating

	Daily and weekly	Tips
Alcohol	1 unit = 125ml wine ½ pint of regular strength beer, cider or lager 1 pub measure of spirits Men – weekly intake < 21 units, with at least 3 alcohol-free days. Women – weekly intake < 14 units with at least 3 alcohol-free days.	If you do indulge, go for a glass of wine watered down with soda or sparkling mineral water.
Dairy	3 portions a day. Milk on cereal, a matchbox-sized piece of cheese or a small pot of yoghurt all count as 1 portion. If in weight-loss mode we recommend up to 284ml, or half a pint of milk per day and no more than 75g low-fat or 50g high-fat cheese per day.	If you don't eat dairy foods remember to make sure you choose calcium-enriched non-dairy alternatives such as soya (look for no-added-sugar versions). You can use any milk you prefer but if you are concerned about your overall fat intake use skimmed or semi-skimmed.
Eggs	1 a day	

	Daily and weekly	Tips
Fibre	4–5 servings (around 18g) fibre-rich foods every day	Soluble fibre = oats, fruits, pulses. Insoluble fibre = vegetables, whole grains, cereals
Fluid	1½–2 litres a day	Can include tea or coffee (try to limit to 3 cups in total) diluted fruit/vegetable juice, herb and fruit teas and water. Alcohol does not count!
Fruit and Vegetables	5 a day – choose as many different colours as possible, and try to divide equally between fruits and vegetables. A 'portion' is generally considered to be 80g.	1 piece of fruit or glass of juice with added water at breakfast. A piece of fruit mid-morning. Some salad or vegetable soup at lunch and 2 portions of vegetables or salad with dinner and you've done it!
Meat	Fresh, good-quality lean meat such as chicken and turkey. Buy organic wherever possible.	Try to keep to a maximum of 3 portions of red meat per week.

	Daily and weekly	Tips
Nuts and seeds	Choose unsalted varieties and go for a good mixture of both nuts and seeds.	30g, or a small handful a day (as a snack or in salads or muesli) will give you a great nutrient boost and has been shown to help keep hunger at bay.
Oily fish	Aim for 1–2 portions a week of salmon, trout, sardines, mackerel, fresh tuna, pilchards, herring, rainbow trout or other dark oily fish.	If you don't eat fish, flaxseeds or omega 3-enriched eggs are good ways of getting your essential fatty acids.
Pulses	3 portions a week in the form of chickpeas, beans (butter beans, garbanzo beans, barlotti beans, low-sugar baked beans, etc.) and lentils.	Add pulses to soups and recipes. Puréed pulses, seasoned with herbs and spices make great dips and spreads. Keep cans of (no-sugar-added) chickpeas or beans on hand for a snack. Rinse and drain, then blend with cumin, garlic, tahini (sesame seed paste) or olive oil and lemon juice for a speedy, healthy dip.

	Daily and weekly	Tips
Salt	Aim to limit salt to a maximum of 6 grams a day or less.	Reduce the amount of processed food you eat, and don't add salt during cooking or at the table.
Saturated fat (within the TOTAL fat amount below)	Men – aim to limit total saturated fat intake to 30g a day Women – 20g a day.	Trim visible fat from meats and remove skin from poultry. Use lower-fat milk and dairy foods. Minimize butter and cream. Use olive oil-based spread instead of butter.
Total fat	Men – aim to limit total fat intake to 95g a day Women – 70g a day	Work on reducing the amount of fats and oils you add when cooking. Don't eat deep-fried foods.

Can I Follow the GL Diet if I'm Vegetarian?

Vegetarians can follow the same healthy low-GL principles as meat-eaters, choosing foods from each of the major food groups, high-protein sources, cereals and grains, dairy products (or soya substitutes), vegetables and fruits. Obviously the more restrictive the diet, the more difficult it becomes to ensure all the body's nutritional requirements are being met. Deciding to follow a vegetarian diet means ensuring that nutrients usually provided by meat or dairy products are obtained from other foods. With some careful consideration, this is easily done.

Calcium

Aim to include three servings of dairy per day. If you don't eat dairy products, choose calcium-enriched soya or tofu, dried fruits such as apricots, green leafy vegetables and nuts and seeds to help meet your calcium requirements.

Iron

Non-meat eaters have to be careful about their iron levels, since the type of iron found in red meat is particularly well absorbed in the body. Other sources of iron include bread, pulses, green leafy vegetables and dried fruits.

Protein

Vegetarians substitute meat with other protein foods such as pulses (lentils, chickpeas and beans), dairy products, eggs and nuts. If you don't eat dairy foods, soya, tofu and Quorn are good protein alternatives.

Vitamin B12

People who exclude all animal products from their diet may develop a deficiency of vitamin B12, so should take a good-quality multi-vitamin and -mineral supplement which includes it, as this vitamin does not occur naturally in plant-based foods.

Zinc

Meat and dairy products are rich sources of zinc, and if you don't eat these you may wish to consider a good quality multivitamin and mineral supplement which includes it.

Main Points to Remember

- Enjoy your food – if you don't like it, don't eat it!
- Eat regularly – every 4 hours is a good guide. Don't skip meals or snacks – you are almost certain to pay for it by overeating or making poor food choices later.
- Eat a good variety of foods – try new things – there are so many fabulous foods out there!
- Get 'slow-carb savvy' and learn to swap high-GL foods for low-GL ones (see page 80).
- Keep hydrated – remember to get $1\frac{1}{2}$–2 litres of fluid a day.
- Try to avoid food with added sugar, glucose, glucose syrups and high fructose corn syrups (not to be confused with fructose). Get your sweetness from fruits and the occasional piece of high-cocoa dark chocolate (70 per cent or more cocoa). Sweeten recipes with natural agave syrup or fructose.
- A lapse is just a lapse, don't turn it into a relapse!

Memory Box
- **Eat every 4 hours**
- **5-a-day fruit and veg**
- **Avoid added sugar**
- **Avoid added salt**
- **Minimum 1½ litres of fluid a day**
- **Eat at least one portion of oily fish a week**
- **Eat a good variety of protein foods**
- **Cut right down on the booze!**

A Week's Worth of Tips

Have a read-through of the tips below to help you get on the right track, then check out the sample weekly plans (pages 15 and 19, and you can also print these from our website, www.dietfreedom.co.uk) to help you manage your weekly food intake.

Breakfast

- Keep a batch of muesli made up for when you are in a hurry.
- Not very hungry? Have a smoothie – a great way of getting some fruit and dairy portions into the day.
- Have a small glass of fruit juice topped up with water if you're struggling with getting your 5-a-day fruit and veg.

- How about some good old-fashioned porridge?
- Choose something yoghurt based – a small portion of yoghurt is 1 of your 3 daily dairy portions for healthy bones.
- Got a bit more time to spare today? Treat yourself to a healthy cooked breakfast (see page 142).
- Feeling decadent? Smoked salmon counts as a portion of heart-friendly oily fish. How about a lazy breakfast of smoked salmon, eggs and rye toast? (See page 165.)

Mid-Morning Snack

- Keep forgetting to have your snacks? Use your mobile, palm pilot or email to send yourself a reminder.
- After a lighter breakfast, a more substantial snack like a couple of oat cakes and some houmous or smoked fish paté will fit the bill.
- Some crudités and a yoghurt or houmous dip will count as 1 of your 5 fruit and veg for the day.
- Got a craving for something sweet? Try 4–5 dried apricots.
- Next time you go to the loo check the colour of your urine – if it's darker than straw, you are not drinking enough water.
- If you miss your snack, you are far more likely to end up in the biscuit barrel or at the vending machine.
- Hey! Don't forget you can eat chocolate! Choose a small portion (2 squares) of dark chocolate with 70% or more cocoa solids.
- Mixed toasted seeds are delicious and nutritious!

Lunch

- How about chickpea salad (page 216) to get 1 of your 3 portions of pulses a week?
- If you're going for something with pasta, remember cooking it *al dente* helps keep the GL lower.
- Don't forget, you don't need to add salt to your food. Use the guide to using herbs and spices in Chapter 5.
- Sandwich on the run? Make it an open one to keep the GL low.
- Never made your own soup? Try our recipe for 'No-fuss Lentil Soup' (page 130) – it's quick to prepare and tastes divine!
- Friends coming round for lunch? Why not whip up a healthy low-GL soup such as the fennel soup on page 124?
- Family roast? No problem, check out our recipes on pages 192–5.

Mid-Afternoon Snack

- A matchbox-sized piece of cheese counts as 1 of your 3 portions of dairy foods a day.
- Keep a bowl of fruit on your desk – if it's under your nose you're more likely to eat it!
- 30g of unsalted nuts has been shown to reduce hunger later in the day.
- Guacamole makes another great topping on an oatcake or rye cracker, and counts as another portion of veg.

- Cottage cheese is a great dairy source and tastes great with fresh pineapple or mango.
- How's that fruit bowl looking? About ready for topping up?
- Getting fed up with oat cakes? Try rye crispbreads such as Ryvita with some sugar-free peanut butter for a change.

Dinner

- Fancy something fishy? A 120-g portion of oily fish counts as one of your 2 portions for the week.
- If you are going to struggle to get time to make lunch tomorrow, make a little extra tonight so you've got some leftovers. The Crustless Spinach Tart (page 186) is great for this.
- When you're choosing meats, select the leanest cuts and ask for any visible fat to be trimmed.
- Out to dinner tonight? Make sure you have all your meals and snacks today, and order a large glass of water to sip while you look at the menu – trust us, it really helps!
- When shopping for fruit and veg choose as many different colours as possible to get the best mix of protective antioxidants – 'Eat a rainbow' every day!
- Fancy rice tonight? Try pearl barley as an alternative, or mix some lentils with the lower-GL brown or wild rice.
- We all like the odd night chilling in front of the TV. Try our Pork with Mustard Sauce and Pasta dish on page 116.

Sample Weekly Plan for Meat-eaters

This is to give you an idea of how to put together a healthy low-GL week.

*Where the following are mentioned in the sample plans below, recommended portion sizes are –

- MEN: oatcakes/crispbreads up to 4, bread up to 2 slices
- WOMEN: oatcakes/crispbreads up to 2, bread 1 slice

	Day 1	Day 2	Day 3	Day 4	Day 5	Day 6	Day 7
Breakfast	Melon & orange smoothie (page 95)	Zesty yog-pot (page 147)	Poached eggs on toast	Orange spice porridge (page 140)	Coconut & apricot energy shake (page 101)	Mushroom 'toast', scrambled egg & bacon (page 142)	Smoked salmon & eggs with rye toast (page 165)
Mid-morning Snack	Oatcakes with cream cheese and cucumber	1 apple	Small handful of toasted seeds	1 pear	Small handful of unsalted nuts	1 orange/ satsuma	Small handful of cherries or grapes
Lunch	Broccoli & almond soup (page 106)	Perky egg & asparagus (page 107)	Hot dressed salad (page 149)	Pumpkin & coconut soup (page 104)	Prawn cocktail wrap (page 222)	Walnut & goat's cheese salad (page 212)	Roast chicken dolcelatte (page 193)

	Day 1	Day 2	Day 3	Day 4	Day 5	Day 6	Day 7
Mid-afternoon Snack	Small handful of dried apricots	Small handful of toasted seeds	Small handful of dried cranberries (sugar free)	1 pot of cottage cheese	Matchbox-sized piece of cheese	Oatcakes with houmous	1 peach
Dinner	Tuna steak with butter beans (page 114)	Steak, mushroom & red pepper stir-fry (page 115)	Salmon & tomato with lime sauce (page 112)	Chickpea salad (page 216)	One-pot pork & orange casserole (page 169)	Roast turkey (page 192)	Fennel soup (page 124)

Sample Weekly Plan for Vegetarians

This is to give you an idea of how to put together a healthy, low-GL week.

	Day 1	Day 2	Day 3	Day 4	Day 5	Day 6	Day 7
Breakfast	'Feelin' fruity' yog-pot (page 117)	Banana and strawberry smoothie (page 118)	Apple & hazelnut muesli (page 119)	Apricot & almond smoothie (page 120)	Pear & pumpkin seed yog-pot (page 121)	Tofu & sunflower smoothie (page 122)	Hot apple porridge (page 123)
Mid-morning Snack	Small handful of toasted seeds	Oatcakes with sugar-free peanut butter	1 apple	Carrot batons with sour cream and chive dip	Small handful of cherries	Celery sticks with houmous dip	Choccie craving drink (page 226)
Lunch	Chicory with watercress & orange (page 125)	Spinach, avocado, pea & mint salad (page 126)	Grilled asparagus with feta cheese (page 127)	No-fuss lentil soup (page 130)	Spinach & cheese soufflé (page 128)	Spicy aduki bean soup (page 131)	Beanie casserole (page 138)

	Day 1	Day 2	Day 3	Day 4	Day 5	Day 6	Day 7
Mid-afternoon Snack	Small handful of grapes	Matchbox-sized piece of cheese	Small handful of dried apricots	Small pot of cottage cheese	Oatcakes with red pepper pate	1 pear	Avocado houmous with cucumber sticks
Dinner	Spicy tofu (page 132)	Spicy vegetable dhal (page 136)	Eastern vegetables (page 133)	Hot vegetable stir-fry with coconut milk (page 134)	Bulgur and butternut squash (page 137)	Cheese and mushroom tortilla (page 139)	Grilled veggie wrap (page 221)

Now It's Your Turn!

Once you have read the book thoroughly including the healthy eating guidelines and looked through the recipes and snack ideas to see which appeal, you are ready to fill in your first low-GL week!

Use a pencil so you can re-use the blank template on page 284. Don't worry, you don't have to fill this in every week (!) but it's a great exercise to get you thinking about a balanced low-GL diet. It will help you to start to 'think low GL'.

Obviously, most of us don't have the time or inclination to make up recipes for all meals – so use quick, healthy alternatives whenever you wish, again based on the guidelines throughout the book.

Chapter 2

WHAT AFFECTS A FOOD'S GL?

Portion Size

To calculate the GL of a food you need three pieces of information:

- The tested GI of the food
- The portion size
- The number of grams of carbs in the portion.

You then simply divide the GI number by 100, then multiply that figure by the number of grams of carbs in the portion.

Example

If a food has a tested GI of 50 and a 100g portion contains 10 grams of carbs:

50 divided by 100 = 0.5
0.5 x 10 carbs = a GL of 5

If you eat two 100-g portions of that food, the GL would double to 10.

- 10 GL or less is classed as low
- 11–19 GL is medium
- 20+ GL is high

The GL is a far more accurate reference than the GI alone because, it takes into account a food's tested GI response in the body plus the size of the portion *and* how many carbs are in that portion. So it combines the quality of the carb as well as the quantity to give you the whole picture instead of just part of it.

The GI of a food is the same whether you eat one portion or 10 (!), which makes it difficult to use as a weight-loss tool as it is completely unrelated to portion sizes – a key factor for weight loss and health.

Portions are SO important – even when using the GL – so remember that just because 100g of a specific food has a low GL of 5, if you eat three portions of it the GL becomes 15 (i.e. moderate).

By understanding the GL of foods and choosing mainly low-GL foods, you can eat more food overall in quantity – BUT it's still not a licence to go bananas!

Food Processing

The way a food is processed affects its GL considerably.

Generally speaking, the more processed, the higher the GL. The nearer a food is to its natural state, the lower the GL.

Bread is a good example – the highly refined and processed, fluffy white breads have a higher GL than the wholegrain, darker dense breads.

The whole grains in wholegrain bread slow down the digestive process, so we can say it is a SLOW carb food, whereas white refined breads are digested much more quickly, producing a sharp rise in blood glucose. We call foods like this FAST carbs.

Similarly, the GL of an apple is low – but if you remove the peel, which contains a lot of fibre, and process it into a concentrated apple juice, the GL rises.

Food Additives

There are many E numbers and enzymes added to foods during processing, either to enhance taste or texture and/or to prolong shelf-life.

We don't know yet exactly how each of these additives affect the GL, but chances are they have an impact, so again, the less tampered with a food is, the better. If a food label starts to sound like a chemistry lesson … our advice is to leave it on the shelf!

Cooking Methods and Times

The GL has been shown to rise after a food is cooked, which makes sense as the food will generally become softer and more easily digested, meaning it will break down into glucose more quickly once eaten, causing a faster rise in blood sugar levels.

Pasta is a good example. If you cook it until it's *al dente* (firm to the bite), the GL will be lower than if you cook it until it is soft.

Raw food is best wherever possible and safe. If you have to heat it, do so gently and don't boil the life out of it or burn it to a crisp!

Ripeness and the Age of a Food

The more ripe or aged a food becomes, the more starches and sugars are released, so it makes sense that a new, baby potato has a lower GL than a large baking potato, and that a ripe banana has a higher GL than an under-ripe one.

Eat baby vegetables when possible, and fruits when slightly under-ripe rather than over-ripe to help keep your GL score as low as possible for the day.

Adding Acidity

Tests have shown that if you add acidity such as lemon juice or vinegar to a high-carb meal it can lower the glycaemic response by up to 30 per cent. This is believed to be because acid slows stomach-emptying and therefore the rate of digestion.

Red wine vinegar and lemon juice have been shown to have the greatest effect when added to foods. It is thought that the body's low-glycaemic response to yoghurt and sourdough breads is due to their high acidity.

Another good reason to use vinegar is that researchers in Sweden have found that vinegar may help us to eat less and reduce the cravings induced by blood-sugar spikes after meals. Interestingly, they found a direct link between increased vinegar intake and satiety (feelings of fullness and satisfaction) after eating.

So, no excuses, get those fresh lemons and vinegars out, add some olive oil and start making a GL-lowering concoction … and no, before you ask, this doesn't mean that you can now eat chips floating in vinegar with impunity!

Fibre Content

There are two types of fibre – soluble and insoluble.

Insoluble fibre helps move bulk through the intestine, which together with fluid and being active helps relieve constipation and has been linked with a reduction in the incidence of colon cancers.

Vegetables and many fruits and root vegetables contain fibre only in their skins, so try not to remove them wherever possible.

When insoluble fibre is finely milled and processed it allows enzymes to cause rapid digestion, thus taking away the added fibre benefit. This is why you will find that some wholemeal breads, 'brown' breads, pasta and rice, despite looking less refined and being higher in fibre, have a very similar GL to their white counterparts.

Wholegrains, flaxseeds and oat fibre are all good sources of insoluble fibre.

Soluble fibre is a gummy mass when mixed with water, and binds with fatty acids which can help lower total and LDL ('bad') cholesterol, reducing the risk of heart disease. It also prolongs stomach-emptying and therefore your feeling of fullness. From the GL standpoint, it slows the release and absorption of sugars into the body and therefore helps regulate blood sugar levels.

Soluble fibre is found in whole oat products and oat bran, legumes, flaxseed, fruits, vegetables and psyllium husk.

Do add extra fibre to your meals and recipes wherever possible, to harness its many benefits – and don't forget to keep hydrated to help the fibre do its job.

Adding Fat and Protein

Adding fat to a food can lower its GL, as it can slow the rate of stomach-emptying and therefore the speed at which a food is digested.

However, this *isn't* a licence to add butter to everything!

A good rule is to try and ensure you have a combination of healthy fats, proteins and carbs on your plate. The fats and proteins will help to moderate the effects of the sugars in the carbs, so that overall you should have a lowish GL effect.

Different Types of Foods

Not all foods within the same family will have the same GL. Different types of potatoes, rice and oats have varying GLs, for instance, as they contain different starches which affect the level of starch gelatinization that takes place, and consequently the GL. Not all foods have been tested yet for their GL. We give you the basics in this book, but if you want more specific and up-to-date low-GL food lists, see www.dietfreedom.co.uk.

Chapter 3

HEALTHFUL OILS AND FORGET-ME-NOT FATS

OK, so some fats are GOOD – despite our 20-year indoctrination that ALL FAT is the devil's work, we have finally cleared that one up once and for all (or at least the latest research has).

Virtually ALL dieticians, health professionals and researchers worldwide nowadays agree – it is the *type* of fat you eat that counts, not just the overall quantity.

Fat is essential in our diet, and the majority of it should come from natural oils from **seeds, nuts, olives** and **fish**. These healthful oils are anti-inflammatory, help protect us against heart disease, improve the condition of our nails, hair and skin, can ease depression, and may even help fight cancer.

Types of Fat

Unsaturated Fats – Eat and Enjoy a Good Variety

Monounsaturated – olive oil, avocados, nuts and seeds
Polyunsaturated – seeds, nuts and their oils, oily fish such
as mackerel, tuna and salmon

Saturated Fats – Eat in Moderation

Found in butter, hard cheeses, coconut oil and fatty meats

Trans Fats – Avoid!

Hydrogenated margarines are made by converting
vegetable oil into fat at very high temperatures, to make
them last longer. Check labels and avoid anything containing trans/hydrogenated fats, as they have been linked with
heart disease and cancer. You will find them in many
commercially-produced baked products and in processed
foods, although countries around the world are now legis-
lating to restrict or ban their use.

What are Essential Fatty Acids (EFAs)?

Fatty acids are the basic building-blocks of all fats and oils. Some of these can be made by the body. The ones the body can't make have to be obtained through the food we eat, and are called **Essential** Fatty Acids (EFAs). They are 'essential' because without them we would die!

EFAs affect our mood, behaviour, intelligence and emotions, and are vital to the functioning of the immune system. A lack of them has been linked to depression, chronic fatigue syndrome and, in children, ADHD (Attention Deficit Hyperactivity Disorder), dyslexia and dysphasia.

Signs of deficiency include dry skin, cracked heels, brittle nails, hyperactivity, joint problems, hair loss, dry eyes and digestive disorders.

Good Sources of EFAs

Foods that are rich in EFAs are fish, nuts, seeds, beans, pulses, and vegetable oils.

What are Omega 3, 6 and 9?

Essential fatty acids are polyunsaturated and split into two groups – Omega 3 and Omega 6.

We need both Omega 3 and Omega 6 in our diet, but achieving the right balance of these is not always easy.

Many scientists believe that an imbalance of these fatty acids is a major reason for the high incidence of heart disease, diabetes and even some forms of cancer.

Our ancestors evolved on a diet with a ratio of about 1:1, but dramatic changes in our diet mean that today's typical diet provides a ratio closer to 24:1 in favour of Omega 6.

The perfect ratio of these oils is believed to be nearer 5:1 in favour of Omega 6. Most people get enough Omega 6, but it is more difficult to get enough Omega 3 from a modern diet.

Omega 3

The essential Omega 3 fatty acid, ALA, is crucial for brain and eye development, helps prevent abnormal heart rhythms, is important for the immune system and reduces blood-clotting. Two other common Omega 3s are EPA and DHA.

Fish and fish oils are probably the best sources of EPA and DHA, but the content varies depending on the species of fish. The best fish sources are salmon, herring, fresh tuna, pilchards, mackerel and sardines.

All dark green leafy vegetables contain Omega 3, as do some plant-derived oils such as pumpkin seed oil, flaxseed oil and walnut oil.

Omega 6

Omega 6 lowers total blood cholesterol levels as well as 'bad' cholesterol (LDL) and is found in cereals, eggs, poultry, wholegrain breads and oils such as sunflower, corn, soya and evening primrose.

Omega 9

Omega 9 is not an essential fatty acid, because humans can make it in limited amounts. It is found in almost all natural fats. Avocados, macadamia nuts, apricot seeds, almonds and olive oil are good sources. Omega 9 helps to prevent cancer and boosts the immune system.

Cooking with Oils and Fats

Cooking at high temperatures can damage oils. The more Omega 3 an oil contains, the less suitable it is for cooking. The heat not only damages the fatty acids, it can also change them into harmful substances. The oils that are higher in saturated fats or monounsaturates are the most stable when heated. Best cooking oils and fats are butter (in small amounts), olive oil-based spreads, olive oil, sesame oil and groundnut (peanut) oil. The main thing to remember when it comes to heating any oils is never to reheat them, as this is when the maximum damage is done.

To preserve the nutritious properties and the flavour of oils you might like to try the 'wet-sauté' method practised by some chefs. Add a couple of tablespoons of water to the pan, heat just below boiling, add the food and cook it lightly before adding the oil, stirring frequently. This shortens the time the oil is in contact with the hot pan. Never heat oils to smoking point, as this damages the fatty acid content and affects the taste adversely. You can still use the more fragile oils at room temperature for dressings.

Storing

Dark bottles are best, as clear glass or plastic bottles allow light to penetrate the oil and oxidize the fatty acids in a chemical process similar to rusting. Store in a cool, dark place and keep the lid on tightly between uses, as contact with air will affect the quality of the oil. Purchase in small quantities and use within a month or two if possible. The healthier the oil, the shorter its shelf-life. Unrefined oils spoil more easily when exposed to warm temperatures, so they need to be refrigerated if you are not going to use them straight away. An exception is olive oil.

Organic

It's definitely worthwhile paying extra for organic oils. Many oils come from plants that are sprayed with pesticides, which are usually fat-soluble, and thus concentrate in the oil portion of the plant. One of the safest oils is extra virgin olive oil, which is not refined or deodorized.

Try and incorporate a variety of oils into your diet, but remember they contain on average 120 calories per tablespoon, so use sparingly. All fats and oils have no GL score as the carb count is negligible.

Avocado oil

History: Avocado seeds were found buried with a mummy dating back to the 8th century BC.

Health bite: Use extra-virgin, cold-pressed. Contains vitamin E and Omega 9.

Everyday uses: Salads or use instead of butter with mashed vegetables.

Coconut oil

History: Coconut oils were recognized as 'health oils' in Ayurvedic medicine as far back as 4,000 years ago.

Health bite: Look for virgin coconut oil. Rich in lauric acid, antiviral, antibacterial and antifungal. A saturated fat, so less likely to be damaged when heated.

Everyday uses: Cooking at high temperatures. Very long shelf-life at room temperature.

Flaxseed oil (or linseed oil)

History: Flaxseed is an ancient grain. Hippocrates wrote of using flax for relief of stomach pains in 650BC.

Health bite: Rich source of Omega 3 and excellent source of protein, potassium and beta carotene. May help constipation and IBS.

Everyday uses: Delicate nutty flavour, add lemon juice or vinegar for dressings. Keep refrigerated. Short shelf-life. Not suitable for cooking.

Groundnut oil (peanut oil)

History: The peanut originated in Brazil. In 1890 in America it was promoted as a replacement for the cotton crop destroyed by the boll weevil.

Health bite: Contains high levels of plant sterols which research shows may protect against colon, breast and prostate cancer.

Everyday uses: Cooking – especially stir-fries. Has a neutral taste and high burn point.

Hazelnut oil

History: The word hazel comes from the anglo saxon word *haesel* meaning 'bonnet', referring to the shape of the outer shell. Hazelnuts have been cultivated in China for the last 5,000 years.

Health bite: Rich in Vitamin E.

Everyday uses: Nutty, rich and flavourful. A little goes a long way. Use in salad dressings with a bit of olive oil, goes well with asparagus. Can be used in baked goods.

Olive oil

History: The olive dates back to 17th century BC and was mentioned in Egyptian records and several times in the Bible. It has been a sign of peace and truce for millennia.

Health bite: Heart healthy. Doesn't need high temperature or chemical processing, since it is made from the flesh of the olive and not the seed. Look for extra-virgin olive oil as it comes from the first pressing of the olives and is therefore the highest quality.

Everyday uses: Any salad dressings; try mixing with balsamic or red wine vinegar. You can cook with extra-virgin although it is more expensive. Fine for medium-temperature cooking but don't overheat. Good shelf-life.

Pumpkin seed oil

History: First recorded reference in Austria 1739. Gourmets have appreciated the culinary and health properties of this delicacy for centuries.

Health bite: Healthy monounsaturated fat, helps increase HDL (good cholesterol) and high in zinc.

Everyday uses: Adding flavour to soups, salad dressings. Try mixing with olive oil, mustard and apple vinegar.

Rice bran oil

History: A newcomer on the block. Production first started in the US in 1960s.

Health bite: A good healthy alternative oil. Great source of vitamin E, antioxidants and micronutrients. Studies in 1990s have demonstrated it helps reduce cholesterol levels.

Everyday uses: Salads. Also has a very high smoke point, so ideal for pan- and stir-frying. Foods cooked in rice bran oil absorb less oil during cooking. Excellent shelf-life.

Sesame oil

History: Babylonians used it for making exotic perfumes, cooking, sesame cakes and as a medicine. A purchase of sesame oil was recorded on an Egyptian clay tablet in King Nebuchadnezzar's palace records in 6th century BC.

Health bite: High in vitamin E. Dark in colour with strong, distinctive flavour.

Everyday uses: Add small amount to stir-fries at end of cooking time, use in salad dressings, or drizzle over steak. Not suitable for cooking. Long shelf-life.

Walnut oil

History: Around 2,000BC, clay tablets in Mesopotamia revealed the existence of walnut groves within the Hanging Gardens of Babylon. Produced in France, where it is well loved and used widely.

Health bite: Very high in Omega 3.

Everyday uses: Salad dressings: combine it with olive oil. Goes well with fruit, cheese and walnuts, often used with fish. Not suitable for cooking. Short shelf-life.

Flavoured/Infused Olive Oils

- **Chilli** olive oil – great with mozzarella cheese, tomato sauces or chocolate
- **Garlic** olive oil – good for sauces, pasta, vegetables, fish or meat
- **Basil** olive oil – goes well with rice and pasta salads, soups and tomato sauces
- **Rosemary** olive oil – use with potatoes, fish, beans, risotto or chocolate
- **Lemon** olive oil – ideal for mayonnaise or with white or red meat or tomatoes
- **Ginger** olive oil – good for soups, fish, meat, rice and cakes
- **Porcini mushroom** olive oil – use in risottos, sauces, soups and with vegetables

Chapter 4

GROOVY GRAINS AND FRIENDLY FLOURS

What Are Wholegrains?

When grains are milled or refined, the bran (the fibre-rich outer layer of the kernel) and germ (the nutrient-rich inner part) are removed, leaving only the endosperm (the middle starchy bit). Most of the nutritional value of the grain is lost in the process, because the bran and the germ contain the highest concentration of nutrients.

To increase your intake of whole grains:

- Eat porridge which is made from wholegrain oats instead of highly refined cereals. Oats, in general, are a great food choice.
- Swap white bread for wholegrain rye/pumpernickel or soya and linseed bread.
- Try eating tabbouleh, a popular dish made with bulgur wheat.
- Use pearl barley (great as a rice substitute, as rice is a high-GL food).

■ Substitute white flour for flours that are less processed
   and contain more fibre such as buckwheat flour, spelt
   flour, soya flour or gram flour.

When looking at food labels, look for the word 'whole' in
front of the name of the grain, for example 100 per cent
whole wheat. Even popcorn is classed as a whole grain!
   Eating healthy wholegrains fits in very well with your
new low-GL eating plan, as wholegrains have a lower GL
than their highly processed counterparts.

Why Eat Them?

Recent research shows that eating wholegrains can help
maintain the health of your heart. You will get more
benefits from eating wholegrains as it is the combination
of all three parts of the grain that provide the best health
benefits.

Which Wholegrains Are Low GL?

■ Bulgur
■ Buckwheat
■ Corn on the cob and unsweetened popcorn
■ Oats (porridge oats makes a great brekkie!)
■ Pearl barley

- Quinoa – if you stick to 30g it brings the GL down to around 9, so is classed as low.
- Rice generally has a high GL, but wild rice and brown rice tend to have a lower GL than most other varieties – use sparingly or mix half-and-half with pearl barley or beans and pulses until you reach your target weight.
- Rye
- Spelt – this is an ancient relative of wheat, and anecdotally (not clinically proven) may be better tolerated than wheat by those with a wheat intolerance. Wholegrain spelt flour has a higher protein and fibre content than most wheat flours, and breads containing spelt have been tested as having a low to moderate GL.
- Wheat – 30g of wholewheat has a low GL of 8.
- Gram flour (chickpea flour) – chickpeas have a very low GL, so gram flour and foods containing it should have a lowish GL too.

Why We Can't Test Flours for Their GL

Glycaemic testing involves volunteers eating an amount of a specific food that contains 50 grams of carbohydrates, three times! Eating that amount of flour is neither palatable nor advisable and, as you can imagine, volunteers are in short supply!

This is why we can only test foods containing specific flours (such as bread containing spelt flour) which will give us the GL of a portion of spelt flour bread.

Combining Flours – How to Get the Right Mix

It's the gluten in wheatflour that makes bread rise, and as many of the alternative flours don't contain as much gluten, you will end up with a denser, heavier loaf, which is a good thing GL-wise, as light and fluffy tends to equal quickly digested and therefore high GL.

By using alternative flours such as rye, spelt and buckwheat in a mixture with stoneground 100 per cent wholemeal wheatflour, you can create delicious bread variations, a little different in taste and texture from sliced white. Actually they taste far better!

Oats are another great addition to try in the form of oat bran, oatmeal or porridge oats, which give bread a lovely texture. We've also used oatmeal with great success as a crunchy crumb coating for fish and meat.

A generous handful of seeds such as linseeds, sunflower seeds or pumpkin seeds in your bread adds to the flavour and will also help lower the GL.

Sourdough breads have a low GL in general, which is thought to be due to the acidic nature of the bread.

Buckwheat flour makes great pancakes – you'll find a recipe on page 110.

Nut flours are very handy in baking, but not much good in bread. They are not as 'sticky' as normal flour (because they have no gluten) and you will find that the finished result will be a little more delicate, yet very tasty! Don't forget that nuts are high in calories, and you shouldn't be eating any more than a small handful a day.

Remember that the more refined and processed a flour is, the higher the GL. The coarser the flour, and the more intact it is (i.e. it has not had all its nutritious parts refined away), the better it will be for you not only in terms of having a lower GL but also with regard to its nutritional content. That is why 'stoneground' wholemeal flour is better than 'brown' or 'wholemeal' flour. By using the stoneground method of processing, the grains stay more intact.

Thickening

In reality, a spoonful of refined cornflour or plain flour here and there wouldn't be too bad if you don't have anything else, but we have banished them from our kitchens and here is what we use in their place!

- Arrowroot – this is available in the baking section of most supermarkets. It's a ground root, as the name suggests, and is great for thickening. There are instructions on the packet, but in general you just use it the same way you would cornflour (mixing with cold water to a smooth paste before adding to anything). As it has no taste or colour this is our thickener of choice for pretty much all sweet and savoury applications.
- Gram flour (chana dhal, besan or chickpea flour) – this is made from chickpeas and is a very popular ingredient in Indian cuisine, which makes a good savoury flour and thickener.

- Xanthan gum – this is an effective thickener although a bit fiddly. It needs a lot of whisking as per the packet instructions and does go lumpy very, very quickly! It's not as easy to find or use as arrowroot.
- Buckwheat flour is a reasonable thickener, however don't use in delicately flavoured foods as it has a stronger taste and so won't work with everything.
- You can replace high-GL white flours with stoneground 100 per cent wholemeal flour in most recipes.
- Spelt flour is also a good thickener. Used exactly as per normal white flour, it's great for soufflés and cheese sauces.
- Organic stock cubes and bouillon powder such as the Marigold and Kallo brands make great gravies, but we love them as warming savoury drinks too! Make sure you choose organic versions, as non-organic often have hydrogenated fats in them. You can also find low-salt varieties.

A Gluten-free Diet?

What is low GL AND gluten free? This is a bit tricky, as many gluten-free products do have a lot of high-GL ingredients and are heavily refined.

Gluten-free corn pastas are generally high GL, so best avoided. However there are some lovely buckwheat (which is actually part of the rhubarb family!) and chickpea pastas available now (see our website for stockists).

Chickpea (gram) flour is a brilliant gluten-free alternative for savoury dishes. It works well as a binder and thickener with strong savoury flavours.

Spelt flour does contain a small amount of gluten.

Soya flour can be used as a gluten-free flour substitute, however it does have a strong taste which is not palatable to everyone.

Being allergic to wheat is not the same as being allergic to gluten, and so you may be able to eat rye, barley, spelt and oats if it is only wheat that causes you problems.

If you have ANY food allergies or medical conditions you need to check with your doctor *before* you make any significant changes to your diet. Take this book with you and ask his or her advice before you start.

Chapter 5

HOT HERBS AND SEXY SPICES

We don't add any salt to our recipes, as we all tend to consume far too much as it is. You will find black pepper and other fragrant herbs and spices in the recipes in this book, though, added for their taste, aroma and also, in some cases, their claimed health benefits.

As we are all different in our likes and dislikes, the herbs and spices are very much optional, so don't be put off a recipe if it has a herb or spice that you don't like – just leave it out or add a different one!

There are no hard-and-fast rules as far as we are concerned as to which herb or spice has to 'be seen' with a certain food. Experiment – you may be as surprised as we are what combos work really well and become future favourite dishes.

Before we start with the recipes, we thought you might like a list of the most popular, easy-to-find herbs and spices, with some traditional uses plus some fresh ideas and combinations for you to try out. We also love a bit of history, and couldn't resist adding bits here and there with some quaint little anecdotes – hope you don't mind!

The health properties of herbs and spices are not to be dismissed. Though many of these are anecdotal and not clinically proven, centuries of medics and cooks cannot be ignored!

Top 10 Herbs

Herbs are wonderful things, with amazing properties and a pretty racy past! Doctors, druids, wise women and chefs have been using these plants for centuries to heal, cleanse, repair, boost and flavour.

You don't have to be a green-fingered gardener to enjoy herbs – you can buy them in pots and pluck with impunity, or grow them from seed yourself. Tina likes to buy them in bunches and freeze them, which works really well, Deborah likes to grow them on the kitchen windowsill and talk to them as she cooks! And we all love the trusty dried herbs in handy shakers.

You can also now buy herbs and spices in convenient tubes and jars, some of which are great, though some do have added sugar and other additives, so always read the label (and see our website for stockists).

Basil

Fresh is best.
Easy to find.
Doesn't freeze well.
Dried is OK.

History: Originally from Indian where it is regarded as sacred to the Hindus; also widely used in ancient Rome, Greece and Egypt.

Health bite: A digestive aid, and also a tonic (just the smell will pep you up!). Also used as a stimulant to aid concentration and help combat weariness.

Traditional uses: Basil was taken as a tea to aid digestion, and for a time the dried leaves were made into snuff to combat headaches and colds! Much used in Italian cooking, it goes beautifully with tomatoes, and if you're into growing your own these make great growing partners, too.

A new twist: All variations of basil (sweet, purple, lemon, etc.) are delicious and augment any dish, from salads to our own 'barleyotto' recipe (page 190). Tear them and add to vegetables and olive oil before roasting. Basil has a delicious flavour and is one of our favourite leaves.

Chives

Fresh is best.
Dried is OK.
Freezes well in water in ice cube trays.

History: Chives have been cultivated for over 5,000 years, and are thought to have originated in China.

Health bite: Chives are reputed as a general tonic.

Traditional uses: Chives have always been associated with egg dishes, cream cheese, fish & chicken.

A new twist: Add at the last minute to literally anything! A liberal sprinkling of fresh chives and a squeeze of lemon juice gives incredible zing to almost any dish we can think of, particularly steamed veggies.

Coriander (cilantro)

Fresh is best for the leaves.
Seeds are dried – best to crush them as and when needed.

History: Aphrodisiac! It has long been reputed to aid *amour*, and was also used in parts of Arabia to ease labour pains and regulate the reproductive system.

Health bite: The essential oil is used to combat poor circulation, digestive problems and colds/flu. Coriander seed tea is used to aid digestion.

Traditional uses: Most used in China, Thailand, Mexico, the southern Mediterranean and the Middle East. Often added to curries, pickles and breads.

A new twist: Stir the leaves through couscous or bulgur wheat, sprinkle on grilled halloumi, use instead of basil to make a pesto, add as a leaf to salads for extra zing. Crush the seeds, and warm in a pan, pour over 1 tbsp of olive oil and use as a warm dressing for halloumi cheese.

Fennel

Fresh is best.
The seeds are dried and can be crushed or added whole.

History: A Mediterranean native, it was brought to Northern Europe by the Romans. One of the 9 sacred herbs of the Anglo Saxons, it is surrounded by much myth and a favourite of the 'white witch'.

It has a reputation for helping eyesight, and was also mixed with straw in kennels and stables to keep away fleas!

Health bite: It is still used by some herbalists to relieve dry tired eyes, earache, toothache, asthma, coughs (it's in many cough mixtures, and gripe water) and rheumatism. It is also a digestive aid and mild laxative.

Traditional uses: The seeds were used in pasta, bread and biscuits to help with the digestion of these starchy foods. The leaves were traditionally laid as a bed upon which to bake a whole fish, gently infusing it with the slight aniseed flavour.

A new twist: Braise the chopped bulbs in white wine for a lovely side dish, or use in place of onion in stir-frys and roasted vegetable combos. Drink the tea made from infusing the seeds as a digestive aid instead of coffee after a meal. Add the finely chopped leaves – only a teaspoon or so – to salads. Fennel is particularly good with oily fish.

Garlic

Fresh is best.
Smoked garlic is wonderful!
Tubes and jars are great but check for added sugar or nasties.
Dried is a good store cupboard standby.

History: Garlic was much used by the Romans, who would chew on raw garlic before battle! Its properties have been lauded by famous literati, including Shakespeare, Chaucer and Pliny. It has been acknowledged for centuries as a plant with great health benefits.

Health bite: Garlic is a natural antiseptic and has blood-cleansing properties. It helps battle colds and flu and boosts the immune system.

Traditional uses: As an intestinal 'cleanse', to lower blood pressure, get rid of worms, alleviate chest infections, and help with the symptoms of rheumatism. In the First World War, the raw juice was used on wounds as an effective antiseptic.

A new twist: Roast whole cloves in their skin (or an entire bulb!) with your next roast, and then squeeze out the sweet cooked garlic – it is truly a magical flavour. Infuse a bottle of olive oil with garlic by peeling and slicing the garlic into the bottle. Use a few drops of this with some lemon juice as a salad zinger or as a great pre-cook marinade for chicken or fish.

Thyme

Fresh is best.
Freezes well.
Freeze loose in bags and you'll find the leaves will easily shake from the stalks, making it very convenient.
Dried works well too.

History: Another Mediterranean native, which absorbs the sun better than most other plants and is packed with medicinal qualities. Has been traditionally used for centuries in pies, stuffings, stews and patés.

Health bite: Thyme has been used for the treatment of colds, coughs, colic and cramps. It is also a digestive and appetite stimulant. An infusion makes a good mouthwash.

Traditional uses: Garden thyme is most traditionally used in the 'mixed herbs' blend (with sage and marjoram) and also in 'bouquet garni' with parsley, marjoram and bay. Garden and lemon thyme are the two most often used in the kitchen, though there are many ornamental varieties that look wonderful and smell incredible in the garden.

A new twist: It makes a great bed on which to bake chicken pieces, and augments tomato-based sauces very well. Add the fresh leaves to salads, sparingly, or mix in with the dressing. You can infuse a light wine vinegar with lemon thyme for a wonderfully fragrant salad dressing.

Parsley

Fresh is best.
Easy to find.
Freezes well.
Dried doesn't work very well.

History: In Greek mythology, parsley sprung from the blood of the hero Archemorous, the forerunner of death – so it was important in their burial rituals. Warriors fed their chariot horses parsley. It is thought to originate in Sardinia. Old wives have it that it thrives only in the gardens of dominant women!

Health bite: The foliage of both the flat and curly parsley is packed with vitamins A, B & C and iron. Parsley tea is given to aid circulation and digestion and to assist the kidneys.

Traditional uses: All parts of the plant are useful, with the roots and larger stems being traditionally blanched and eaten as vegetables. The seeds have also been used in the making of cheese – though the seeds are rarely used now. Parsley stalks are often included in 'bouquet garni'.

A new twist: Add to salads in abundance with other leaves and herbs for a vitamin packed and tasty alternative. It is a fresh-tasting and mild herb, so can be used for colour in almost any leafy setting. Add fresh, finely chopped leaves to mashed veggies.

Mint

Fresh is best.
Easy to find.
Easy to grow.
Freezes well.

History: Stories of mint date back to Greek mythology and biblical times when it was strewn liberally on floors for its sweet cooling scent and insect-repelling properties as well as being used to scent bathwater. In Saxon Britain it was known as 'the monk's herb' as it was so well used by them.

Health bite: Peppermint, spearmint and lemon mint all make a very refreshing and uplifting tea. It is a digestive and may help calm the stomach after meals or when feeling delicate. It will help unblock the sinuses, and is also renowned as a natural aid to a deep, restful sleep. It is also said to have a beneficial cumulative effect in building up a resistance to colds.

Traditional uses: All varieties of mint were reputed to stop milk from curdling. Leaves of the 'eau de cologne' mint were added to the bath for a cooling experience. It is also used in Benedictine, crème de menthe and Chartreuse.

A new twist: In the summer make iced peppermint tea – pour hot water over fresh mint, and let steep for a while, then top up with cold water, strain, add ice cubes, fresh mint leaves and refrigerate. Use mint generously in salads, with freshly steamed veggies. Mint and freshly squeezed pomegranate juice makes a great salad dressing. Try tossing watermelon and feta cheese chunks with lots of torn fresh mint leaves, some lemon juice and a little olive oil.

Rosemary

Fresh is best.
Easy to find.
Easy to grow.
Freezes well in a bag, coming easily off the stalk when you need it.
Dried is a good standby.

History: Considered a magic and sacred herb in many cultures.

Greek students used to weave rosemary in their hair in ancient times while studying for exams. It has also long been used as a natural insect repellent.

Health bite: Rosemary is used in hair tonics and anti-dandruff shampoos to stimulate the scalp, encouraging shiny, healthy hair. It is used as a herbal cure for 'nervous' headaches. It has a 'bracing' aroma and is great added to your bath in the morning to aid consciousness!

Traditional uses: Oil of rosemary was used in the original 'eau de cologne'. Rosemary is also a traditional plant of remembrance, used in Australia on Anzac (Remembrance) Day as a buttonhole. Traditionally it is used with lamb and heavy meats, however while it is a strong herb, it's a lot more versatile than that, so don't be afraid to experiment!

A new twist: Add 2 tablespoons of fresh chopped leaves to any low-GL bread recipe for a lovely pungent lift to your morning toast! Add some freshly chopped rosemary to any pasta or bean dish, particularly if using tomatoes. It goes very well with steamed cabbage – put a sprig of fresh rosemary into the steamer first, then steam the cabbage on top of it. Wash the leaves and dry carefully – add to olive oil or light vinegar for a wonderful dressing/marinade standby.

Sage

Fresh is best.
Freezes very well.
Dried is a good standby.

History: Sage is another Mediterranean native, reputed to be one of the magic ingredients for eternal life! Was used by the Egyptians to boost their intellectual powers and revive a tired brain after much exertion.

Health bite: Reputed to aid memory and help boost energy levels. It is a very well-known antiseptic ingredient used in mouth washes and gargles. Can also help alleviate indigestion and heartburn. Sage tea can be taken as a tonic for the liver and the nerves.

Traditional uses: Sage has been used in tea, in cheeses, breads and hair tonics (apparently stops you going grey!) for centuries. It was also traditionally used with pork, duck and goose. It works well in cheese dishes, and is used in cheese production.

A new twist: If you're feeling sluggish have a cup of sage tea in the morning – made with fresh or dry leaves. A sprinkling of finely chopped sage in any salad is lovely. It goes very well with fresh tuna or other oily fish – sprinkle fresh chopped leaves over the top, or incorporate dried sage into a dressing. It also goes well with eggs, cheese, tomatoes and gives a lift to vegetable soups (especially pea soup). A generous handful inside a roast chicken imparts a lovely flavour.

Top 10 Spices

The fate of countries and dynasties have risen and fallen with spices. Use of spices can be traced as far back as 3500BC to the ancient Egyptians, who used them not only in food but also in cosmetics and for embalming their dead.

King Solomon's vast wealth was attributed to spices. The Chinese were very enterprising spice-traders, dealing with Arab traders who went to great pains not to pass on their jealously-guarded spice routes to their customers.

While the dominant trading power in the Mediterranean changed from Egypt to Babylon and then Assyria, the Arabs held on to their role as the suppliers of these exotic wares for many years. Incredible stories were told by these canny traders about snake-infested pits of cinnamon and mythical, vicious winged birds that guarded various spice crops.

It was the Romans who introduced spices into Northern Europe.

The religious Crusades started the spice wars, and spices were, for a time, more precious than gold and silver due to their rarity.

Marco Polo was first to dispel the myths about fearsome beasts guarding the spices. His book, written while in prison, inspired future generations of spice traders.

The year 1400AD brought the so-called Age of Discovery and a Europe-wide obsession with finding the best spice route to the East. Vasco da Gama from Portugal was the first round the Cape of Good Hope, coming home to Lisbon with trade agreements and a ship laden with spices. Christopher Columbus found the New World, bringing home chillies, allspice and vanilla as well as chocolate, maize and peanuts. Magellan and Drake both made their names – and incredible discoveries – in the name of spice!

The Dutch and British soon took over, and their bloody battle for spice supremacy lasted nearly 200 years.

Today we take these readily available exotic ingredients for granted, and it is very hard for us to imagine a time when a handful of cardamoms were worth more than some people's annual wage!

Next time you use a spice, it's worth remembering that the fate of nations and many lives have hung in the balance over them – their taste and aromas have launched many ships, sparked huge exploration and they have, in fact, played a major part in the shape of the world as we know it today.

Allspice

The best flavour comes from the whole seeds ground as you need them.

History: Allspice is the berry of a tree native to the West Indies and Central America. It is also known as Jamaica pepper or pimento. The dried berries of this type of myrtle tree are very hard and smell of a combination of cinnamon, nutmeg and cloves.

Health bite: The essential oil of the berries and leaves are used in preparations for flatulence and are also antiseptics.

Traditional uses: Allspice is almost always ground, and was traditionally used in mulled wines, fruit cakes, fruit and steamed puddings as well as an integral part of many spice blends. Many Scandinavian and German dishes use allspice.

A new twist: Add a $\frac{1}{2}$ teaspoon of ground allspice to mashed squash or sweet potatoes, or mix into some olive oil and drizzle over before you bake these veggies. Put a teaspoon in with a meatball mix, or in with a winter stew. Add a teaspoon to some fine oatmeal, some black pepper, mix well and use as a crispy coating for fried herring.

Chilli

There are so many types of chillies it's hard to say which are best – choose your favourites, fresh or dried, and approach any unknown chillies with caution!
If you've got a greenhouse or conservatory you can easily grow your own.

History: The chilli is an American native, and there are many different types, strengths and flavours. The Aztecs used to blend cocoa and chilli for a pungent and spicy hot chocolate very far removed from the modern-day version!

Health bite: While rich in vitamin C, you are unlikely to eat enough chilli for that to make a health difference. Chillies do stimulate the appetite and cool down the body, particularly in the hotter climates. If you eat too hot a chilli – yoghurt or milk are the best ways to cool down your mouth quickly.

Traditional uses: Hot dishes, curries, Thai and Mexican cuisine all rely on various types of chillies, from the searingly hot bird's eye chillies to the slightly milder cayenne version. Many milder chillies are dried and smoked and add wonderful warmth and flavour to stews, marinades and sauces.

A new twist: If you get the chance to test different chilli powders or fresh chillies, then do. They can add wonderful depth and pungency to a dish, not just heat. Add a pinch to steamed cabbage, toss with a little olive oil and some garlic for a really fresh side dish. Add a pinch of smoky passilia chillies to a tablespoon of half-fat cream cheese or houmous for a delicious dip.

Cinnamon

It's more pungent if bought in sticks and ground as needed, however it is very handy ready-ground and still tastes great.

History: This exotic spice is made from the ground bark of a tree native to Ceylon (Sri Lanka) and Malabar. It has been much sought-after since biblical times when it was valued above gold. Cinnamon is an ancient herbal medicine mentioned in Chinese texts as long as 4,000 years ago.

Health bite: Has a broad range of historical uses in different cultures. Believed to be helpful for diabetes, colic, indigestion, heartburn and yeast infections. Test-tube studies show that cinnamon can augment the action of insulin. However, use of cinnamon to improve the action of insulin for diabetics has not been proven in clinical trials.

Traditional uses: Mulled wines, stewed fruits, cakes, puddings and biscuits and, more recently, sprinkled on coffee in coffee bars.

A new twist: A teaspoon of cinnamon in your porridge in the morning will give it a real lift. Include cinnamon instead of sugar in your coffee, or use a cinnamon stick as your coffee stirrer for an aromatic brew. Put a pinch in winter stews for wonderful warmth.

Cardamom

Best bought in pods and split/crushed as needed.

History: Cardamom bushes reputedly grew in the Hanging Gardens of Babylon.

Health bite: Cardamom cools the body, and aids digestion. It has been used for millennia as a tooth-whitener and breath-freshener. It is used in Ayurvedic medicine as a cure for urinary tract and skin complaints.

Traditional uses: Indian curries, sweetmeats and ice cream all employ cardamom, and it's used a great deal in Scandinavian cooking. Arabian coffee is often brewed with or poured through cardamoms.

A new twist: Include a sprinkling of cardamom pods in the gravy for any roast meat. Split the pods, crush the seeds and sprinkle in with beans, rice, our own 'barleyotto' recipe (page 190). Also adds an extra dimension to stir-fries.

Cumin

Best bought as seeds and 'dry fried' for about 30 seconds before adding to anything, or crushing as it improves the flavour.

History: Cumin comes from Egypt and has been found in the pyramids. It has been grown for centuries in the Mediterranean, the Middle East and India, is mentioned in the Bible, and was very popular in the UK in the Middle Ages.

Health bite: Widely reputed to be good for the stomach. Also much used in veterinary medicines, and the oil is used in perfumes.

Traditional uses: One sniff will tell you it is another traditional ingredient in curry powder. It is also used in Moroccan and Mexican cooking.

A new twist: Cut one pack of halloumi cheese into thin slices, toast a teaspoon of cumin seeds in a hot pan, add 1 tablespoon olive oil and then fry the halloumi until golden. Add to stews, or crush and mix with olive oil and brush on meat before grilling.

Ginger

Fresh is definitely best, and it freezes in chunks (don't bother to peel) making it very quick and easy to grate and always have on standby. Dried ginger has a deeper, warmer flavour and is used in sweet baking.

History: Ginger is king of the spices in our book! Its first mention on the page appears to be in the writings of the Eastern philosopher Confucius in 500BC. Henry VIII was a fan, and the renowned herbalist Culpepper also sang its praises.

Health bite: Renowned for anti-nausea properties, and great for the digestive system. Also aids absorption, often used in Chinese medicine to speed the absorption of the herbal remedies prescribed. Also known to help reduce fevers and warm away colds.

Traditional uses: Crystallized and powdered in sweet cakes and biscuits and fresh in Chinese cookery. It is also used widely in Indian cuisine.

A new twist: Add about 1 tsp fresh grated ginger, a pinch of hot chilli flakes and a clove of crushed or grated garlic to a pan, add 40g cooked brown rice per person, and a handful of butterbeans. Stir-fry for about 2 mins, then serve as a delicious spicy side dish to most meats.

Mustard

Seeds, ready-made, powder – choose your favourite and enjoy it! Avoid ready-made mustards that contain flour.

History: White mustard is native to Europe, and Black mustard, which is hotter, to Asia and Africa. A mustard paste was recommended by Pythagoras as a treatment for scorpion stings.

Health bite: Mustard baths and footbaths were said to ease all manner of muscular aches. It is reputed to be good for the respiratory system.

Traditional uses: Although mostly grown for the seeds, mustard greens have been eaten in salads or as a spinach alternative for centuries. Ground mustard powder is another staple part of many curry blends. It is traditionally served with beef.

A new twist: Add grainy mustard to cauliflower mash. It really complements the flavours of oily fish, mushrooms and cheese. Spread thinly over rye bread and drape with smoked salmon.

Nutmeg

Buy whole and grate as needed to keep the flavour at its most pungent.

History: The popularity of nutmeg hit its zenith in the 17th century, and only started to wane in the 19th century. The tongue-twister 'Peter Piper' relates to nutmeg and mace (same fruit), and a Frenchman called Peter Poivre who successfully broke the monopoly the Dutch had taken from the Portuguese in the trading of nutmeg and mace in the 1700s.

Health bite: Reputed to cure flatulence and assist the digestion of rich foods. Nutmeg is an astringent, a stimulant and, apparently, an aphrodisiac.

Traditional uses: Traditionally has been used with eggs, cheese and spinach as well as in sweet products such as biscuits, custards and spicy cakes. It is also one of the ingredients in traditional mulled wines. The oil is also used in perfumes and ointments.

A new twist: Grate over wilted spinach. Grate into mushroom or pumpkin soup. Grate over vegetables before roasting, particularly squash. Grate into your cauliflower mash. Grate into stewed apple. Grate a little into your hot chocolate or coffee.

Paprika

Paprika is most often found powdered.
Smoked paprika is wonderful, too.

History: From the same family as the chilli and a native of America. The large, aromatic capsicums are dried and ground. Though grown in many countries, the best quality is said to come from Hungary and is known as 'Noble Sweet'. Paprika is also known as 'Grains of Paradise'.

Health bite: Although rich in vitamin C there are no other notable health benefits associated with paprika – so enjoy it just for its wonderful warmth and flavour!

Traditional uses: Hungarian goulash, paprika chicken. It is also very popular in Spanish and Portuguese cooking. It is a very common commercial flavouring and colouring agent.

A new twist: Paprika, through 'smoked paprika' is enjoying something of a revival currently, and its warm smoky flavour brings welcome depth to cheese, chicken, egg and fish dishes.

Pepper

Peppercorns in a mill freshly ground as you need them retain far more flavour and pungency than ready-ground pepper.

History: Originally from the East Indies, all colour berries come from the same plant. The Romans used it a great deal because it was a relatively cheap spice. Rents in the Middle Ages were often paid in peppercorns due to their high value and scarcity, and the term 'peppercorn rent' at that time meant payment in full.

Health bite: It is said to be good for anaemia, a sluggish digestion, nausea and stiff joints, and to be a real tonic to help oust colds and flu.

Traditional uses: Traditionally, white pepper was used for white food, black pepper for 'coarse' food. It was also used as a meat preservative. Pepper is now the most widely used spice and works well in almost any dish – including some fruit!

A new twist: Freshly ground black pepper for all things! Experiment with fruit, such as strawberries with finely ground pepper; or with figs and goat's cheese.

Chapter 6

LOW-GL SWEETNESS

Yes, we could say banish all sweetness from your life, but we aren't going to for several reasons – (all sweet-lovers punch air at this point) – the first one is that sweet is nice … and savoury, albeit delightful, can be a bit of a bore when it's your only choice.

If you cast your mind back to the low-carb diets, when meat, fish, eggs, cheese and chemical sweeteners or 'run to the loo' polyols were the order of the day … what boring days they were.

So you will be pleased to hear that we aren't going to ask you to banish ALL sugars from your diet and replace them with nasty-tasting chemical alternatives, which may or may not have side-effects – the jury still being out on that one. And we certainly don't want to take the risk of replacing one 'not great for you' ingredient for another. Besides, we wouldn't advocate anything that we don't eat ourselves or don't believe to be good for you.

So where does that lead us – can we really have sweetness *and* goodness, or are the two mutually exclusive? Well, we have scratched our heads over this one for many a moon – how to find sweetness and goodness with a low GL?

Fruit is a great sweetener – chop it, squeeze it, purée it, liquidize it and generally shake it about; add it to porridge, muesli, yoghurt, fry it in olive oil and add it to savoury dishes – and if it is low-GL fruit (and most of them are), all the lovelier.

At this point you may be thinking how you hate washing the blender, or haven't got one, or have got one in the loft, competing for dust with the cappuccino machine and the ice cream maker … and that every time you have bought fresh fruit in the past it has been discovered sitting at the back of the fridge with a furry coat on a week later.

Fear not. You can buy puréed fruit now with no added sugar (see our website for stockists) plus you can get some nice fruit juices (some mixed with veg) without added sugar, too – so you won't have to do anything except tear off the top and pour – quite painless in fact. So we can all have some sweetness in our lives with good old-fashioned fabulous fruit.

'But,' say the clever cooks amongst us, 'we can't bake without sugar … it's … it's *unheard* of!' Well, good news: YES YOU CAN and should. The empty calories in sugar aren't the only way we can make things taste and look good. Our current best of the best available now that are sweet AND good are:

Agave syrup – a delicious, natural low-GL sweetener made from the same plant that tequila comes from. It has fewer calories than sugar, is sweeter (so you can use up to a third less), takes less time to cook AND has a low GL. It is much thinner than honey, so is easy to use and 'pourable' from a bottle. Apart from being brilliant for baking and desserts, you can also use it in porridge, added to yoghurt, or it mixes easily with cocoa to make a delicious low-GL chocolate syrup/sauce (see page 252 for recipe). It isn't widely available in the UK but see our website for stockists.

You can now buy **crystalline fructose** in the supermarket, which has a much lower GL than sugar and, as it's a third sweeter, you can use less. Use on its own or mix with fruit purée to replace sugar in baking.

Don't confuse *'fructose'* with *'high fructose corn syrup'* which is a high-GL sweetener used by the food industry.

The Low-down on Polyols (Sugar Alcohols)

These sweeteners are being added to more and more so-called low-carb products by the day, and recently some products claiming to be low GI/GL, but you need to be aware that they are controversial, as are the 'net carb' claims used on packaging.

Manufacturers are putting the actual carb count in very small print on the back of the product (polyols are high in carbs) but then claiming that you don't need to count them as carbs – hence the low 'net carbs' figure. Their reasoning is that polyols are digested differently to normal carbs and therefore can be discounted; however, this is still a controversial issue, particularly as there are numerous different types of polyols on the market, all with varying effects.

The main issue, however, is that they can cause some very unpleasant side-effects – namely chronic wind and emergency dashes to the loo! If you have IBS then they are best avoided, as they can seriously aggravate it.

The main polyols used worldwide are:

- xylitol
- erythritol
- HSH (hydrogenated starch hydrolysates)
- isomalt
- lactitol
- maltitol
- mannitol
- sorbitol.

Polyols are chemical reductions of starches and sugar molecules, but they are, in fact, neither sugar nor alcohol.

The term can be confusing, as 'sugar alcohols' are not digested like sugar, nor do they have the same effect as alcohol. For this reason, in the US they are now lobbying the Food and Drug Administration (FDA) for an official name change so that consumers are not misled.

Polyols are carbohydrates, but their different chemical structures affect how thoroughly we absorb them. Polyols break down slowly and are incompletely absorbed from the small intestine into the blood, because there is no specific transport mechanism in the body for their absorption. Some of the polyols are absorbed and some broken down in the large intestine and metabolized into short-chain fatty acids, which are then absorbed and used for fuel (and which count as calories).

Intestinal bacteria ferment the rest, producing gases which can cause gastrointestinal distress, followed by strange sounds, bloating and sometimes diarrhoea. Any undigested part of the polyols is excreted. Products containing polyols must carry a warning – 'Excess consumption may have a laxative effect'. All polyols have the capacity to produce intestinal discomfort.

As there appear to be differences in the way different polyols are absorbed, we all have a different level of tolerance to them. Some people may experience gastrointestinal discomfort after eating as few as 10 grams – and a single serving of a polyol-sweetened product could include twice that amount. If you eat several foods containing polyols throughout the day, the grams soon stack up and you can end up with a very embarrassing problem!

So, treat foods containing polyols with caution, and bear in mind that although there are different types, consuming too many polyols is likely to cause gastrointestinal distress. You may also find that relying on 'net carbs' as trumpeted on labels is not a good indicator as to the food's effect on your body or weight-loss efforts.

Many other artificial sweeteners such as aspartame are low GL, but we will leave it for you to decide whether you want to include them in your diet or not. Personally we avoid them as they aren't natural and are controversial health wise.

If you want to buy a sweet treat, look for natural products sweetened with a *small* amount of fructose, natural honey or agave syrup, as these should have a lowish glycaemic impact without any side-effects.

Chapter 7

GENERAL GUIDELINES FOR SUCCESS

Swapping High-GL Ingredients for Low Ones

You will find no sugar or white flour in any of our recipes. Both are replaced with lower-GL, less processed and less refined, more natural substitutes. You won't find any added salt, either, and you won't need it! We do, however, like our herbs and spices ... a lot – and use them instead of salt as a great taste-enhancer. They also have lots of health benefits and colourful histories, as you've seen in Chapter 5!

Thankfully the food industry is now taking an interest in producing ingredients that have a low GL, so the choices are ever-expanding. Until recently the major concern was the fat and calorie content of foods, but this is changing rapidly. Now the focus is moving towards ingredients and products that have a low GL, do not contain unhealthy hydrogenated or trans fats, are low in salt, have no added sugars and are as natural and unprocessed as possible. Wholegrains are also becoming a health focus as research proves their nutritional and health benefits.

It may take some time, possibly years until we have low-GL substitutes for all of the high-GL, highly processed ingredients now out there, but we have made sure that the recipes in this book are as natural as possible and that they are ALL low GL.

So you don't need to worry about anything, we have done all the working out for you so you can just follow the recipes – enjoy your scrumptious low-GL meals and lose weight (or just feel better) as a welcome side-effect!

We have also put together a low-GL 'swapping list' for you – so you can see at a glance some of the ingredient substitutes you can make. Do experiment to find your favourite mixes.

Your Swapping List

High GL (avoid)	Low GL (try instead)
Sugar (brown and white) *See Chapter 6*	❑ small amount of fructose or, our favourite, agave syrup *(not widely available – see www.dietfreedom.co.uk for stockists).* *Fructose is not the same as high-fructose corn syrup, which is a highly processed, high-GL ingredient to be avoided.* *No more than a dessertspoon of agave OR fructose per day.*

High GL (avoid)	Low GL (try instead)
White flour *See Chapter 4*	❑ whole grain flour ❑ oat flour ❑ soya flour ❑ nut flours (such as almond, walnut, etc.) ❑ gram flour *(made from chickpeas, does have quite a strong savoury taste so you may want to use sparingly or mix with other flours)* ❑ buckwheat flour ❑ spelt flour ❑ stoneground wholemeal flour *Again, although generally products made with these flours will have a lower GL than products made with highly processed white flours, they are still high in carbohydrates so use only in moderation.*
White bread	❑ darker, denser wholegrain bread ❑ soya and linseed bread ❑ sourdough bread ❑ pumpernickel/rye bread *Women, no more than 1 slice per day; men, no more than 2 slices per day while in weight-loss mode.*

High GL (avoid)	Low GL (try instead)
Potatoes	❑ new potatoes
	❑ sweet potatoes
	❑ yams
	❑ other vegetables
	❑ beans and pulses
	An average portion would be 80g. Don't exceed this amount of potatoes in a day.
	Recent research shows that cooking potatoes and refrigerating them before eating lowers the GL, as does adding a vinegar-based dressing.

High GL (avoid)	Low GL (try instead)
White rice	❑ pearl barley
	❑ buckwheat
	❑ wild rice
	❑ brown rice
	Only eat small portions of rice – no more than a
	handful – combine with beans or pulses
	❑ chickpeas
	❑ butterbeans
	❑ pinto beans
	❑ haricot beans
	❑ cannellini beans
	❑ lentils
	any beans or pulses or a 'combo' of the above –
	whichever you have in the cupboard!
Pasta (white)	❑ chickpea pasta
	❑ buckwheat pasta
	❑ mixed beans & pulses
	❑ wholewheat pasta *(no more than a handful)*
	vegetable pasta – julienned vegetables, blanched,
	drained and served with pasta sauce

High GL (avoid)	Low GL (try instead)
Ripe fruit	❑ firm, less ripe fruit – this has a lower GL *The vast majority of fruits are low GL – tropical fruits tend to have a higher GL than others such as berries. The less processed and closest to their original form, the better.* *The fibre in the skin (where edible) helps to slow the rate of digestion and the glycaemic response.* *Ripe bananas have a far higher GL than unripe.*
Milk Chocolate	❑ dark chocolate with 70%+ cocoa content and minimal sugar *Combine agave syrup with cocoa to make a delicious, natural, low-GL chocolate sauce – see recipe page 252.*
Cornflour/ wheat flour as thickeners	❑ Arrowroot, which works in the same way as cornflour and is available from almost all supermarkets in the baking section. *Use as per instructions on the packet.*

Food Notes

Milk

Your choice! Choose from cow's, goat's, sheep's or soya milk – you can also use coconut milk, oat milk and nut milk for a change. Up to half a pint or 284ml a day. You can choose which milk you prefer to use, but bear in mind that the recipes are based on using semi-skimmed cow's milk, so if you use something else the results may vary slightly.

Yoghurt

All yoghurts without added sugars have a low GL. Choose a natural, sugar-free yoghurt, bio-yoghurt or Greek yoghurt. If you are concerned about your saturated fat intake then use low-fat yoghurt versions, just make sure they have no added sugar. The low-fat natural 'bio' yoghurts are generally more creamy in texture. Aim to eat the equivalent of a small pot of yoghurt every day.

Cheese

All cheese is low GL. As per yoghurt you can choose lower-fat cheeses such as Edam or ones that state 'low or reduced fat' on the packaging. They generally taste really good. If you prefer full-fat cheese, just limit the amount used. Don't eat more than 75g of low-fat or 50g of high-fat cheese per day.

Herbs

Herbs and spices won't add to your GL. You can use either dried herbs or the puréed herbs in tubes (check they have no sugar or additives) instead of fresh in most recipes, although the results may not be quite as good. Freezing fresh herbs works really well. See Chapter 5 for the low-down on herbs and spices, and remember that if you don't like a herb or spice in a recipe, swap it for something you do – or omit them altogether if you prefer.

Fats

Fat doesn't add to your GL score. In fact, both fat and protein eaten at the same time as carbohydrates help to slow down the speed of digestion and therefore lower your glycaemic response to the overall meal.

Use either olive oil or olive oil-based spreads (no trans/hydrogenated fats) for frying and baking. A small amount of butter is fine now and then if you prefer.

Vegetables

Virtually all vegetables have a low GL – so enjoy! An average portion would be around 80g. Just avoid normal white potatoes – try to use new potatoes or sweet potatoes instead. Again, 80g would be a sensible portion, and you should aim for three portions of vegetables per day.

Fruit

Most fresh fruit has a low GL. Ripe bananas are one exception, so just go for a small banana that is yellow-and-green striped instead.

Some dried fruits such as dates, figs, raisins and currants have a high GL, so are best avoided. Go for dried apricots, apple, mango and cranberries instead, but make sure they have no added sugar. One or two portions of fruit a day (alongside your three vegetable portions) is ideal.

Meat and Fish

All meat and fish is carbohydrate free so won't add to your GL. Follow the healthy eating guidelines in Chapter 1 regarding meat and fish.

Nuts and Seeds

Both are very good for you but very calorie dense, so limit to a small handful a day if you want to lose weight.

Should We All Buy Organic?

You can follow a low-GL diet by buying 'everyday' foods, and many people do just that because the cost of buying organic plus lots of 'special' ingredients can mount up. But it has to be said that, for some foods, switching to organic makes a lot of sense.

Organic foods are becoming more and more popular every year as we all become increasingly aware of the food that we eat, where it comes from and, in the case of animals, how they were treated and what they were treated with (i.e. antibiotics and hormones) prior to arriving on our plates. Consumers are becoming more demanding as factory farming and the methods used to fatten animals ever faster and more profitably are now under the media spotlight in a big way.

The food we buy nowadays can come from practically anywhere in the world, so it makes perfect sense to be cautious about what we choose to eat and what we provide for our families.

Many supermarkets are now offering a wider range of organic and cruelty-free foods, so do check them out and, if in doubt – ASK!

If buying all organic is a bit of a financial stretch, at least try to buy organic meats, poultry and organic or free-range eggs.

Organic meat comes from animals that have been raised using more traditional methods, hence the higher cost. It tastes far better and will be free from antibiotic residues, which is important for our future health. Conventional farmers often add antibiotics to animal food to make animals grow faster, so when we eat the meat we absorb many of the antibiotic residues, which could cause future problems as we are becoming more and more resistant to all sorts of antibiotics. The fewer antibiotics you are exposed to, the fewer you'll be resistant to.

So even if you have to buy smaller portions to keep the cost the same, your body will thank you in the long run!

If you can stretch to organic fruit and vegetables as well, even better, as you will avoid the chemical residues and get more nutrients for your money. Mineral levels of organic fruit and vegetables can be 100 per cent higher than non-organic, and they contain less water than those grown using fertilizers and chemical sprays, so you get far more quality and less water for your money. It's a sobering thought that the fruit and veg you eat as an individual each year will probably have been sprayed with a gallon of herbicides and pesticides!

You may have noticed that a lot of fruit and vegetables are quite tasteless nowadays. This is due to their high water content. Some tomatoes taste just like water, and the same goes for some apples!

With food, as with most things in life, you get what you pay for – make cutbacks elsewhere, but making the quality of the food you eat your priority is the best thing you can do for your own and your family's health.

If animal welfare is something you care about, look for foods with the blue-and-white 'Freedom Foods' label which is run by the RSPCA. It is the only UK farm-assurance scheme dedicated to improving standards of animal welfare. If you visit their website www.freedomfood.co.uk you can see how your own supermarket is performing in this regard. You will also find links and listings for local farmers' markets, farm shops and organic box schemes in your local area.

The world's top chefs use organic produce in their restaurants for the quality and taste. If you haven't tried organic meat, fish or poultry – try it, you won't go back!

Convenience and Canned Foods

Canned food is a great store cupboard standby. Just check for added sugars and salt. Even canned vegetables such as peas and carrots can have sugar added!

Canned fruit is OK providing it isn't in a sugar-laden syrup. Fresh fruit is obviously better but if you do buy cans look for the ones in their own juice with no sugar added.

Baked beans are probably the most popular canned food, but again, they all have sugar added. You can get cans of organic baked beans sweetened with a small amount of apple juice. See our website for stockists. The same rule applies to any other convenience foods. Check the labels for added sugar and choose organic where possible.

Chapter 8

7-DAY RECIPE SELECTOR

We are all deliciously different!

No two people reading this book are the same, and neither are we, so we have split the recipes up into different sections. Tina is the 'fast and friendly' recipe fiend – her criteria being 'if it tastes good, looks good, is healthy AND can be thrown together in a few minutes, marvellous and all the more enjoyable!' You won't find any of Tina's recipes taking more than 20 minutes start to finish, as Tina (and we are sure a few of you out there, too) has reached her boredom threshold by then!

Deborah, on the other hand, finds cooking a relaxing and soothing thing, a form of therapy even, so she is more than happy to peel and chop and stir and marinate for as long as it takes to get to the end result. Deborah has devised the 'foodie-friendly' recipes, so be prepared for a bit of prep work here and a bit more time spent.

Both of us are very keen on vegetables, so we have combined our approaches to create the 'veggie-friendly' recipes.

Nigel is kind of in-between depending on his mood and the time he has to spend (not that he is moody, you understand!).

And we'd like to take a minute here to thank Diet Freedom online Club members Andie, Olivia, Lorraine, Selina, Caroline, Sally and Lesley for kindly passing on some lovely recipes to us which we have included in the chapters to come.

For you, some of the recipes and ingredients will have immediate appeal, and others you may wrinkle your nose at – just play around until you get into your own GL groove, so to speak.

Don't forget that if you need more help and guidance you can **take a look at www.dietfreedom.co.uk to check out the many services we provide to keep you bang up to date on GL and healthy eating.**

In all the recipes, tsp = teaspoon, tbsp = tablespoon, and dsp = dessert spoon.

Chapter 9

FAST AND FRIENDLY RECIPES

Breakfast

Melon and Orange Smoothie

Preparation: 5 minutes, Serves 1

½ small melon, peeled, deseeded and chopped
1 large orange, peeled and chopped (pips removed)
1 lime, juice only
handful of fresh mint (optional)
2 tbsp natural, sugar-free yoghurt

Add all ingredients together, blend and serve.

Cranberry and Apricot Muesli

Preparation: 10 minutes, Serves 4

120g/generous ½ cup porridge oats
50g/1 generous tbsp dried apricots
50g/1 generous tbsp dried cranberries (sugar-free)
your choice of milk to serve

Combine all dry ingredients in a bowl. Add desired amount
of milk and serve.

Optional:
Add a spoonful of natural, sugar-free yoghurt.

Cheesy Herby Eggs on Toast

Preparation: 5 minutes, Cooking: 5 minutes, Serves 2

4 large free-range eggs

4 tbsp milk

1 tbsp olive-oil spread

2 tbsp cream cheese

2 tbsp mixed herbs (chives, parsley, oregano or whatever you
    have)

freshly ground black pepper

2 slices of toasted soya and linseed or rye bread

Beat the eggs and milk in a bowl and add black pepper.
Heat olive-oil spread in a frying pan and add egg mixture.
Stir constantly with wooden spoon until the eggs are set
but still soft. Remove pan from heat and stir in cream
cheese, herbs and pepper. Serve on the toasted bread.

Watermelon Smoothie

Preparation: 5 minutes, Serves 1

¼ of a deseeded watermelon cut into chunks
handful of ice cubes
1 tbsp natural, sugar-free yoghurt
2 tsp agave syrup
½ tsp ground ginger

Blend all ingredients together and serve.

Cinnamon and Chocolate Porridge

Preparation: 2 minutes, Cooking: 1–5 minutes depending on method used, Serves 1

30g/2 level tbsp porridge oats
½ tsp cinnamon
2 tbsp/30ml water
1 tsp cocoa
1 tbsp agave syrup

Place porridge and cinnamon in a microwave-safe bowl. Add water. Microwave on full power for 1 minute and stir. Add more water if necessary. Mix cocoa with agave syrup to form a chocolate sauce. Drizzle over porridge. If preferred, you can cook the porridge on the hob in a small saucepan.

Nutty Blueberry Smoothie

Preparation: 10 minutes, Serves 2

4 peaches or nectarines, sliced and stoned
50g/½ cup blueberries, fresh or frozen
50g/½ cup strawberries, fresh or frozen
1 large slightly unripe banana, cut into chunks
6 tbsp natural, sugar-free yoghurt
6 Brazil nuts
2 tsp agave syrup

Place the peaches or nectarines into a juicer and extract the juice. Pour the juice into a blender with the remaining ingredients except the agave syrup and blend. Add agave syrup to sweeten if desired. Serve immediately in tall glasses.

Coconut and Apricot Energy Shake

Preparation: 5 minutes, Serves 1

125ml/½ cup coconut milk (no added sugar)
125ml/½ cup natural, sugar-free yoghurt
handful dried apricots, chopped
handful ice
2 tsp agave syrup
55–85ml/¼–⅓ cup your choice of milk

Place all ingredients into a food processor or liquidizer and blend together until combined and smooth. Pour into a tall serving glass and serve at once.

Lunch

Tuna and Bean Oatcakes

Preparation: 5 minutes, Serves 1

2 tbsp kidney beans
1 small can tuna, drained
½ red onion, diced
1 small tomato, diced
handful chopped fresh parsley (optional) or ½ tsp dried
1 tbsp pine nuts, toasted or untoasted
squeeze of fresh lemon juice
2 sugar-free oatcakes or Ryvita

Mix all together, squeeze over the lemon and serve with a couple of sugar-free oatcakes or Ryvita.

Wild Mushroom Omelette

Preparation: 5 minutes, Cooking: 20 minutes, Serves 2

1 tbsp olive oil
100g/2 cups wild mushrooms (or button)
4 large free-range eggs, beaten
freshly ground black pepper
50g/1 cup any hard cheese, grated coarsely
parsley to taste

Heat half the oil in a pan, add the mushrooms and cook for 5 minutes until golden brown; set aside. Heat the rest of the oil in the same pan and add half of the beaten egg. Add black pepper and stir with a wooden spoon, bringing the cooked egg to the centre and allowing the runny egg to go to the edge of the pan and cook. Add a quarter of the mushrooms, cheese and parsley and fold omelette over, making sure egg is cooked through. Place on a warm serving plate and repeat process to make two omelettes.

Pumpkin and Coconut Soup

Preparation: 10 minutes, Cooking: 20 minutes, Serves 4

1 red onion, chopped
1 tsp dried ginger
1 clove garlic, chopped or ½ tsp dried or purée
1 tsp olive oil
1 kg (2.2 lb) pumpkin, peeled and chopped
365ml/1½ cups organic vegetable stock
470ml/2 cups coconut milk (sugar-free)
freshly ground black pepper

Fry the onion, ginger and garlic in the olive oil until soft-ened. Add the pumpkin and cover and sweat on a medium heat for about 10 minutes, stirring occasionally. Add the stock and coconut milk and cook until soft, add more water if required. Add black pepper, blend until smooth and serve.

Tuna and Red Pepper Pot

Preparation: 10 minutes, Serves 2

400g/1½ cups mixed beans

1 small can tuna, drained

1 red pepper, chopped

½ red onion, chopped

1 tbsp sun dried tomatoes, chopped

1 tbsp/15ml extra virgin olive oil

1 tbsp/15ml red wine vinegar

freshly ground black pepper

Drain beans and tuna and mix with red pepper, onion and tomatoes. Combine olive oil, vinegar and black pepper for dressing. Combine altogether and serve in a pot.

Broccoli and Almond Soup

Preparation: 5 minutes, Cooking: 15 minutes, Serves 4

1 onion, chopped
2 leeks, chopped
1 garlic clove, crushed or ½ tsp dried/purée
500g broccoli florets
1.5 litres organic vegetable stock
60g/4 tbsp flaked almonds, toasted
crème fraîche

Fry onion, leeks and garlic in oil until softened. Add broccoli florets and 1.5 litres vegetable stock. Bring to boil and simmer until soft. Blend soup until smooth. Serve with toasted almonds and a spoonful of crème fraîche.

Perky Egg and Asparagus

Preparation: 10 minutes, Cooking: 8 minutes, Serves 2

12 asparagus spears
water
½ tbsp white wine vinegar
4 large free-range eggs
60g/4 tbsp olive oil-based spread/butter
1 lemon, juice only
1 tbsp chopped fresh tarragon or 1 tsp dried/purée

Steam or boil asparagus for about 3 minutes or until just tender. Bring a pan of water to the boil and add the vinegar. Crack eggs in and simmer for a few minutes. Melt the spread/butter in a pan and stir in the lemon juice and tarragon. Place asparagus spears on a plate, top with poached eggs, drizzle with the warm lemon and tarragon dressing and serve.

Bacon Frittata

Preparation: 5 minutes, Cooking: 10 minutes, Serves 1

2 large free-range eggs
1 spring onion, chopped
1 tomato, chopped
freshly ground black pepper
drizzle of olive oil
2 slices lean bacon, chopped

Preheat oven to 220°C /425°F/Gas Mark 7. Beat the eggs in a bowl and mix in the spring onion, tomato and seasoning. Heat the oil in a non-stick ovenproof frying pan and fry the bacon for a few minutes, until golden. Pour the egg mixture into a pan and toss the pan for even cooking. Cook until set and transfer to the oven for 4–5 minutes, until golden brown and cooked through. Remove from the oven and serve.

Dinner

Halloumi Cheese Kebabs

Preparation: 10 minutes, Cooking: 15 minutes, Serves 2

1 tbsp agave syrup

1 tsp mustard

1 tbsp/15ml olive oil

240g (usually one packet) halloumi cheese, cut into cubes

8 cherry tomatoes

8 button mushrooms

1 red onion, peeled, quartered

Preheat oven to 200°C/400°F/Gas Mark 6. Mix together agave, mustard and olive oil. Thread the cheese, tomatoes, mushrooms and onion onto four metal skewers, alternating. Brush the agave/mustard mix over the skewered cheese and vegetables. Place on a baking tray, turning occasionally, and bake for up to 15 minutes or until golden brown.

Buckwheat Crepes with Smoked Salmon

Preparation: 10 minutes, Cooking: 10 minutes, Serves 2

100g/1 cup buckwheat flour

1 free-range egg

250ml/1 cup your choice of milk

125g/generous ½ cup ricotta cheese

1 garlic clove, crushed or ½ tsp dried/purée

2 tbsp chopped parsley

freshly ground black pepper

grated rind of half a lemon

2 tbsp/30ml olive oil

400-g can artichoke hearts, drained and chopped

juice of 1 lemon

250g smoked salmon, cut into strips

Place the flour, egg and a splash of milk in a bowl and whisk until smooth. Gradually whisk in the remaining milk. Mix the ricotta with the garlic, parsley, pepper and lemon rind. Heat a tsp of the oil in a non-stick frying pan; when hot pour off any excess and spoon 3 tbsp of the flour-and-milk batter into the pan. Cook on each side until browned. Transfer to a plate and keep warm. Make three more crepes in the same way, adding more oil if necessary. Divide the ricotta and artichoke between the crepes, drizzle with lemon juice, grind some black pepper over and serve with the salmon.

Salmon with Tomato and Lime Sauce

Preparation: 5 minutes, Cooking: 8 minutes, Serves 4

½ tbsp olive oil

4 large boneless salmon fillets

2 tomatoes, finely chopped

½ red onion, finely chopped

juice and zest of 3 limes

2 tbsp chives, snipped

freshly ground black pepper

Heat the olive oil in a pan and cook the salmon for 4 minutes each side until cooked through. Mix the tomatoes, onion, lime juice, zest and chives together in a bowl and add black pepper. Place the salmon on plates, drizzle with the sauce and serve.

Quick Cajun Chicken

Preparation: 5 minutes, Cooking: 15 minutes, Serves 4

1 tbsp paprika
½ tsp mild chilli powder
4 skinless chicken breasts
1 tbsp/15ml olive oil

Preheat oven to 200°C/400°F/Gas Mark 6. Mix together spices. Toss in chicken breasts and coat lightly. Drizzle oil over a baking sheet and add chicken breasts. Bake for 15 minutes or until cooked through.

Tuna Steak with Butter Beans

Preparation: 5 minutes, Cooking: 8 minutes, Serves 2

400g (usually 1 can)/2 cups butterbeans, cooked
1 red onion, sliced
1 clove garlic crushed or ½ tsp powder/purée
1 tbsp/15ml extra virgin olive oil
½ tbsp red wine vinegar
2 tuna steaks

Combine the butter beans, onion, garlic, olive oil and vinegar and set aside. Brush tuna with olive oil and fry for 4 minutes each side. Arrange butterbean salad on two plates and top with tuna steaks.

Steak, Mushroom and Red Pepper Stir-fry

Preparation: 5 minutes, Cooking: 15 minutes, Serves 4

500g/1 lb lean beef steak
1 tbsp/15ml olive oil
2 red peppers, deseeded and chopped
200g/4 cups mushrooms, sliced
1 clove garlic, crushed or ½ tsp dried/purée
100g/1 cup mangetout
200ml/⅔ cup crème fraîche
1 tsp wholegrain mustard

Cut steak into strips and fry in the preheated oil in a large frying pan or wok for about 5 minutes until the meat starts to brown. Add red pepper, mushrooms and garlic. Cook for a few minutes until softened. Add the mangetout, crème fraîche and mustard, stir and cook for a few more minutes.

Pork with Mustard Sauce and Pasta

Preparation: 10 minutes, Cooking: 10 minutes, Serves 2

200g/4 cups buckwheat, wholegrain or chickpea pasta

1 tbsp olive oil

1 red onion, chopped

1 red pepper, deseeded and sliced

2 large lean pork medallions, trimmed and sliced

Small tub/1 cup of crème fraîche or single cream

1 dsp wholegrain mustard

freshly ground black pepper

water as needed

Boil pasta with a tsp of the olive oil in boiling water until just cooked but still firm to the bite (*al dente*). Drain pasta and set aside. Heat olive oil in a large frying pan. Add onion and red pepper until starting to soften. Add pork, stirring until brown and cooked through. Stir in crème fraîche/cream, mustard and black pepper. Add some water to thin down the sauce. Stir in pasta and serve.

Chapter 10

VEGGIE-FRIENDLY RECIPES

Breakfast

'Feelin' Fruity' Yog-pot

Preparation: 5 minutes, Serves 2

100g/⅔ cup chopped mixed nuts
140ml/½ cup natural, sugar-free yoghurt
1 apple, finely diced
2 tbsp dried cranberries (sugar-free), chopped

Mix all ingredients together in a bowl/pot and serve.

Banana and Strawberry Smoothie

Preparation: 5 minutes, Serves 1

1 slightly unripe frozen banana, cut into chunks
120g/½ cup natural, sugar-free yoghurt
225g/2½ cups fresh strawberries
grated nutmeg (optional)

Combine all ingredients except nutmeg in a blender and purée until smooth and creamy. Pour into a glass and dust with nutmeg.

Apple and Hazelnut Muesli

Preparation: 10 minutes, Serves 4

120g/½ cup rolled oats
100g/½ cup dried apricots, roughly chopped
100g/⅔ cup toasted hazelnuts, chopped roughly
250ml/1 cup fresh apple juice
2 apples, peeled and grated
1 small tub/1 cup natural, sugar-free yoghurt
1 tbsp agave syrup

In a large bowl mix together the oats, apricots and hazelnuts. Pour over the apple juice and leave for 10 minutes to allow the oats and dried fruit to soak up the juice. Divide the muesli between 4 bowls and top with grated apple. Spoon on a dollop of yoghurt and drizzle over agave syrup. Serve immediately.

Apricot and Almond Smoothie

Preparation: 5 minutes, Serves 2

6 fresh apricots (or tinned in natural juice – not syrup)

250ml/1 cup fresh orange juice with bits

200g/1 cup natural, sugar-free yoghurt

1 tsp ground flaxseeds (optional)

2 tbsp flaked almonds

grated nutmeg (optional)

Throw everything together, blend and serve.

Pear and Pumpkin Seed Yog-pot

Preparation: 5 minutes, Serves 1

1 large firm pear, chopped

1 tbsp Greek yoghurt or natural thick yoghurt

1 tbsp pumpkin seeds (toasted if preferred)

Combine the yoghurt and pear. Sprinkle over the pumpkin seeds and serve.

Tofu and Sunflower Smoothie

Preparation: 5 minutes, Serves 1

50g/½ cup soft tofu
1 apple, chopped
250ml/1 cup your choice of milk
1 tbsp sunflower seeds
1 tsp unsweetened cocoa powder
2 tsp agave syrup

Throw everything together, blend and serve.

Hot Apple Porridge

Preparation: 1 minute, Cooking: 1 minute, Serves 1

30g/2 level tbsp porridge oats
1 large apple, finely chopped or grated
2 tbsp/30ml water
2 tbsp natural, sugar-free yoghurt

Place porridge in a microwave-safe bowl. Add water and apple and stir. Microwave on full power for 1 minute and stir. Add more water if necessary. Top with the yoghurt and serve. If preferred, you can cook the porridge on the hob in a small saucepan.

Lunch

Fennel Soup

Preparation: 10 minutes, Cooking: 35 minutes, Serves 4–6

1 medium onion, chopped
30g/2 tbsp olive oil
4 bulbs fennel, chopped
bouquet garni – 3 parsley stalks, 1 sprig thyme, 1 bay leaf, tied
    together
900ml/3½ cups organic vegetable stock
freshly ground black pepper

To garnish:
fennel leaves
lemon zest

In a large pan, fry the onion in olive oil for approx 5 minutes until translucent. Stir in the fennel and add the bouquet garni, stock and pepper. Bring to the boil, cover and simmer for 30 minutes until the vegetables are very tender. Remove the bouquet garni and allow the soup to cool slightly. Blend the soup until it is smooth, either with a hand blender or in a liquidizer. Reheat. Garnish with the fennel leaves and lemon zest and serve immediately.

Chicory with Watercress and Orange Salad

Preparation: 10 minutes, Serves 4

3 heads chicory
3 large oranges
2 bunches watercress
3 tbsp/45ml extra virgin olive oil or groundnut oil
freshly ground black pepper

Trim the chicory, separate into leaves, wash and dry. Put into a salad bowl. Coarsely grate (or use a zester) the zest of one orange, place in a small bowl. Squeeze the juice and add to the zest. Peel the remaining 2 oranges and cut into segments (make sure you have no pith on the segments). Add the orange to the chicory. Trim, wash and add the watercress to the salad. Add the oil and black pepper to the orange zest and juice and whisk together. Pour over the salad, toss and serve immediately.

Spinach, Avocado, Pea and Mint Salad

Preparation: 10 minutes, Serves 2

250g/1 large bag fresh spinach leaves, rinsed and dried
1 large avocado, skinned, destoned and cut into chunks
150g/1½ cups petit pois or peas – fresh or frozen and
    defrosted
1 generous handful of fresh mint
2 tbsp/30ml avocado oil or extra virgin olive oil
1 tbsp/15ml white wine vinegar
freshly ground black pepper
small handful of pumpkin seeds

Put the spinach, avocado, petit pois and fresh mint into a salad bowl. Whisk the oil, vinegar and black pepper together. Pour over the salad leaves and toss well. In a small frying pan, heat the pumpkin seeds over a high heat until they 'pop' and turn golden. Sprinkle over the salad, serve immediately. (If you don't have fresh mint, add a teaspoon of dried mint to the dressing.)

Grilled Asparagus with Fresh Mint and Feta Cheese

Preparation: 5 minutes, Cooking: 4–5 minutes, Serves 2

12 fresh asparagus spears
2 tbsp/30ml lemon juice
2 tbsp/30ml olive oil
freshly ground black pepper
70g/½ cup feta cheese
2 tsp fresh mint leaves, roughly chopped

Preheat grill to a high heat. Trim the woody ends off the asparagus and place on a heat-proof plate. Mix 1 tbsp of lemon juice and 1 tbsp of olive oil and the black pepper together and pour over the asparagus. Place the plate under the grill, turning occasionally, for about 4–5 minutes. Pour any juice left on the plate into a jar; add the rest of the olive oil and lemon juice and more black pepper to taste, put the lid on the jar and shake into a dressing. Cut the feta into chunks. Arrange the cooked asparagus and feta between the two plates, sprinkle with mint, and pour over the dressing. Serve immediately. (If you don't have fresh mint add a teaspoon of dried mint to the dressing.)

Spinach and Cheese Soufflé

Preparation: 5 minutes, Cooking: 40 minutes, Serves 4

30g/2 tbsp olive oil-based spread

25g/1 tbsp spelt flour

150ml/¾ cup your choice of milk

3 large free-range eggs, separated

125g/1 cup frozen spinach, thawed and squeezed dry

50g/1 cup strong Cheddar cheese, coarsely grated

¼ tsp grated nutmeg

freshly ground black pepper

2 tbsp Parmesan cheese, grated

Preheat oven to 190°C/375°F/Gas Mark 5. Grease 4 large ramekin dishes (or one 6-inch/15-cm soufflé dish) and tie a paper 'collar' round each to support the soufflé as it rises. Melt the olive oil-based spread in a small pan, stir in the flour and cook for a minute. Remove from heat and stir in the milk, return to the heat and slowly bring to the boil, stirring all the time. Cook for 3 minutes, then take off the heat and add the egg yolks, spinach, Cheddar, nutmeg, pepper and half the Parmesan and mix thoroughly. Whisk the egg whites until fairly stiff. Using a metal spoon, fold one spoonful of the egg white mix into the spinach mix, then carefully fold in the rest. Transfer to the prepared dishes, sprinkle with the remaining Parmesan cheese. Bake for 15–20 minutes (25–30 minutes if in one large dish) until risen and golden. Serve immediately with a green salad.

No-fuss Lentil Soup

Preparation: 10 minutes, Cooking: 45 minutes, Serves 4

2 tbsp/30ml olive oil
1 medium onion, chopped
2 medium carrots, chopped
3 sticks celery, chopped
1 clove garlic, chopped or grated
4 cardamom pods, split but with seeds left in
125g/1 cup lentils
600ml/2½ cups organic vegetable stock
freshly ground black pepper
fresh parsley to garnish

Heat the oil in large pan, add the vegetables (these or any you like best) and garlic and fry until softened. Add the remaining ingredients. Bring to the boil, cover and simmer for 45 minutes, stirring occasionally. Check the seasoning and serve sprinkled with parsley.

Spicy Aduki Bean Soup

Preparation: 15 minutes, Cooking: 1 hour 15 minutes, Serves 4

150g/1 cup aduki beans, soaked for 3 hours in cold water

2 tbsp/30ml olive oil

1 medium onion, chopped

2 tbsp harissa paste

3 sticks of celery, chopped

2 medium carrots, chopped

2 cloves garlic, chopped or grated

1 can (approx 200g) tomatoes

1 tbsp tomato purée

1 bay leaf

1 tsp fresh thyme, chopped

900ml/3½ cups organic vegetable stock

freshly ground black pepper

handful of fresh parsley, chopped (optional)

Once the beans have been soaking in cold water for 3 hours, drain and rinse. Heat the oil in a large pan, add the onion, harissa paste, celery, carrots and garlic and cook until the vegetables start to soften. Add all the remaining ingredients except the parsley. Bring to the boil and cook on a high heat for 10 minutes, then simmer gently for an hour. Serve with freshly chopped parsley if desired.

Dinner

Spicy Tofu

Preparation: 5 minutes, Cooking: 10 minutes, Serves 2

250g/1 cup firm organic tofu

1 tsp olive oil

2 tsp sesame seed oil

2 tbsp/30ml soy sauce

1 tsp Chinese 5 spice

2 tsp agave syrup

a few sesame seeds for sprinkling over finished dish

low-GL vegetables to stir-fry or steam

Slice tofu into 2.5-cm/1-inch thick slices and dry with kitchen paper. Heat olive oil in a pan, add tofu and cook on both sides for about 10 minutes until it turns golden brown. Combine sesame oil, soy sauce and spices in a bowl. Add the warm tofu, then add the sesame seeds and stir well. Drizzle over the agave syrup and sprinkle a few sesame seeds on top. Serve with steamed or stir-fried vegetables.

Eastern Vegetables

Preparation: 20 minutes, Cooking: 20 minutes, Serves 6

325g/2 generous cups couscous

2 tbsp/30ml groundnut (peanut) oil

2 tsp curry powder

1 tsp cumin seeds

1 large onion, sliced

2 small sweet potatoes, peeled and cubed

4 carrots, sliced

450g/2 cups cauliflower florets

50g/approx 6 dried apricots, cut into chunks

125ml/½ cup water

1 generous handful fresh coriander, roughly chopped

zest of 1 lemon, grated

Cook the couscous as per the packet instructions. Put the oil into a large saucepan (with lid), add the curry powder, cumin seeds and onion, cook until the onion is soft. Add the vegetables, apricots and the water, bring to the boil, cover and simmer until tender. Drain any excess water from the couscous, stir in the coriander and lemon zest. Serve with the vegetables. If you like choose your favourite fresh herb to stir into the couscous.

Hot and Spicy Vegetable Stir-fry with Coconut Milk

Preparation: 10 minutes, Cooking: 10 minutes, Serves 6

2 pieces lemon grass

1 tsp cumin seeds

4 fresh red chillies, deseeded and finely chopped

5-cm/2-inch piece fresh ginger, peeled and finely diced, or 1
    tsp dried/purée

500g/4 cups mixed vegetables, such as broccoli, cauliflower
    florets, aubergines (eggplant), asparagus, carrot, sugar
    snaps, sweet potato, courgettes (zucchini) – all cut into
    slices/chunks roughly the same size

2 tbsp/30ml groundnut (peanut) oil

200ml/1 cup coconut milk (no added sugar)

Trim off the root end of the lemon grass and finely chop the more tender part of the stalk. Crush the cumin seeds and add the finely chopped chillies and ginger. Mix together to form a paste, preferably with a pestle and mortar (though you can also use a small blender to chop and blend the spicy chilli mixture. You may also want to add lime leaves or cardamom seeds to the spice blend). Once your vegetables and chilli paste are ready, heat the oil in a large frying pan or wok over a medium heat. Add the chilli mixture and, stirring continuously, fry for 3–4 minutes. Add the coconut milk and bring to the boil, then add all the vegetables and cook for 5–6 minutes until they are starting to become tender. Serve immediately on warm plates.

Spicy Vegetable Dhal

Preparation: 20 minutes, Cooking: 1hr 10 minutes, Serves 4

250g/1 cup yellow split peas
900ml/3½ cups water
2 large carrots, sliced
½ small cauliflower, cut into florets/chunks
1 medium courgette (zucchini), thickly sliced
1 tbsp/15ml groundnut (peanut) oil
1 large onion, finely chopped
2 garlic cloves, chopped or grated
1 tsp ground coriander
5 whole cardamom pods
1 tsp freshly grated ginger, or ½ tsp dried

Rinse split peas and put into a large saucepan, cover with cold water and bring to the boil. Simmer for about 1 hour or until the peas start to soften – topping up the water as necessary to keep them covered. Add the carrots, cauliflower and courgette and simmer until tender – approx 10 minutes. Heat the oil in the frying pan; cook the onion until softening, stir in the garlic and spices, and cook for a further 3–4 minutes. Drain the split pea and veggie mix, then stir in the onion and spices.

Bulgur and Butternut Squash

Preparation: 10 minutes, Cooking: 20 minutes, Serves 2

1 kg/2.2 lb butternut squash, peeled and diced
200g/1¼ cups of bulgur wheat, cooked as per instructions on
    packet
200g/1¼ cups feta cheese, cubed
handful of fresh sage, chopped or ½ tsp dried
freshly ground black pepper
1 tbsp agave syrup
juice of 1 lemon

Roast butternut squash in oven, covered, at 180°C/
350°F/Gas Mark 4 until just starting to soften. Combine
the cooked bulgur wheat, feta and roasted squash. Add
the chopped sage and black pepper and toss together.
Combine agave syrup with lemon juice, drizzle over and
serve.

Squash also goes well with cinnamon, chilli, coriander
and nutmeg.

Beanie Casserole

Preparation: 15 minutes, Cooking: 25 minutes, Serves 4

1 onion, chopped

1 clove garlic, chopped or ½ tsp dried/purée

150g/2½–3 cups button mushrooms, sliced

1 leek, chopped

1 tbsp olive oil

420g/2 generous cups mixed pulses

410-g can red kidney beans

2 x 400-g cans/4 generous cups chopped tomatoes

50g/2 tbsp Parmesan cheese, grated

250g/2 small parsnips, peeled and grated

Preheat oven to 200°C/400°F/Gas Mark 6. Fry onion, garlic, mushrooms and leek in a pan in the olive oil until softened. Rinse and drain pulses and kidney beans and add to pan. Add tomatoes and heat through. Combine the Parmesan and the grated parsnip. Place the bean mixture in an ovenproof casserole dish. Cover with the Parmesan and parsnip mixture and sprinkle over some olive oil. Bake for 25 minutes or until golden brown and crispy.

Cheese and Mushroom Tortilla

Preparation: 10 minutes, Cooking: 35 minutes, Serves 4

2 tbsp/30ml olive oil
2 medium sweet potatoes, peeled and diced
250g/4–5 cups button mushrooms, sliced
1 leek, sliced
6 large free-range eggs
handful fresh chives, chopped or 1 tsp dried
150g/3 cups mature Cheddar cheese (or any hard cheese),
    coarsely grated

Heat the oil in a medium-sized pan over a medium heat.
Add potatoes and cook for 5 minutes until turning golden.
Add mushrooms and leek and cook until softened. Meanwhile, beat the eggs together in a bowl with 2 tbsp cold
water. Add chives and cheese and pour into the pan. Cover
pan and cook for 15 minutes on a low heat, tilting pan so
that uncooked mixture runs to the outside and cooks. The
tortilla should be set throughout and golden underneath.
Divide into 4 slices and serve warm.

Chapter 11

FOODIE-FRIENDLY RECIPES

Breakfast

Orange Spice Porridge

Preparation: 5 minutes, Cooking: 5 minutes (microwave), 10 minutes (hob), Serves 1

30g/2 level tbsp porridge oats

125ml/½ cup water

1 tsp cinnamon

1 tsp ground ginger (or fresh grated ginger)

zest of half an orange

1 tbsp/15ml freshly squeezed orange juice (or orange juice preferably not from concentrate)

1 tsp agave syrup

1 tbsp crème fraîche

If using microwave:

Put the oats, water, cinnamon, ginger, orange zest and juice in a microwaveable bowl, cook for approx 3 minutes and stir. Return to cook for a bit longer if necessary. Stir in the agave syrup, and dollop on the crème fraîche.

If using hob:

Cook the oats, water and cinnamon in a small saucepan over a high heat, stirring continuously until it reaches the desired consistency. Stir in the agave syrup, and dollop on the crème fraîche.

You can use honey or fructose to sweeten if you don't have agave.

Mushroom 'Toast' with Scrambled Eggs and Smoky Bacon

Preparation: 5 minutes, Cooking: 15 minutes, Serves 2

4 rashers lean bacon
2 large flat mushrooms, stalks removed
15g/1 tbsp olive oil-based spread
4 free-range eggs
freshly ground black pepper

Heat the grill to medium. Put the bacon and mushrooms (top facing up) under the grill. Carefully take the mushrooms out when starting to brown on top, turn over and spread the underside of mushrooms with half the spread, put back under the grill topside-down until mushrooms start to brown and bacon is cooked. Meanwhile, whisk together the eggs with the black pepper in a bowl. Place a small saucepan on a medium heat, add the remaining spread, and when melted add the egg mixture. Stir eggs continuously with a wooden spoon until just scrambled. Take off the heat and fill the underside of the mushrooms with the scrambled egg. Chop the cooked bacon, sprinkle over the eggy mushrooms and serve.

Sweet and Savoury 'No Cook' Breakfast

Preparation: 7 minutes, Serves 1

100g/1 generous slice watermelon, cut into chunks
50g/1 matchbox-sized piece Jarlsberg cheese (or any cheese you have), cubed
1 thick slice of ham, cut into strips (from deli counter – not 'plastic' ham!)
5 strawberries, washed, hulled and halved
handful of blueberries, washed
1 tsp balsamic vinegar

Arrange a layer of watermelon on a plate. Sprinkle the ham and the cheese cubes over the top. Top with the strawberries and blueberries. Drizzle balsamic vinegar over the top and serve.

Cheeky Chocolate Smoothie

Preparation: 7 minutes, Serves 1

water

your choice of milk

1 heaped tsp cocoa (unsweetened)

1 medium firm banana, cut into chunks

1 tsp fresh grated ginger (or ½ tsp ground ginger)

1 tsp linseeds or flax seeds

1 tsp agave syrup (optional)

Using the glass you'll drink your smoothie from, measure the water and milk out, adding half and half so the glass is ¾ full, and add to the blender. Add all other ingredients, blend until smooth and serve.

Apricot 'Jam' on Toast

Preparation: 5 minutes, Cooking: 10 minutes, Serves 4 servings of 'jam' which will keep in the fridge for a few days

100g/½ cup dried apricots

2 tbsp/30ml water

1 tsp agave syrup or fructose

1 slice of low-GL toast (such as soy and linseed)

Chop the dried apricots into very small pieces. Put the apricots, water and syrup/fructose into a small saucepan and bring to the boil. Boil rapidly for a few minutes, but don't let it boil dry! Take off the heat and allow to cool. Spread on the toast. Put the remainder of the cooled jam in a covered pot in the fridge. This jam is also good stirred into yoghurt, or to add a bit of sweetness to porridge or muesli.

Cheesy Puffs

**Preparation: 10 minutes, Cooking: 10 minutes,
Serves 4 (2 puffs each)**

4 free-range egg whites
50g/½ cup ground almonds
½ tsp cream of tartar
30g/2 tbsp fresh Parmesan cheese, finely grated (or can use
    ready-grated)
40g/¾ cup strong Cheddar, coarsely grated, or any other hard
    cheese
1 tsp paprika

Preheat oven to 180°C/350°F/Gas Mark 4. Grease a deep
muffin tin, or use muffin cases. Whisk the egg whites until
stiff and glossy. Mix the ground almonds, cream of tartar,
cheeses and paprika together in a bowl. Gradually fold the
cheese mixture into the egg whites, gently. Divide the
mixture between the 8 tins/cases. Bake for 10 minutes or
until golden. Remove from oven and place on a wire rack to
cool slightly.

These are lovely warm, but also very good cold for a
lunchbox-filler.

Zesty Yog-pot

Preparation: 5 minutes, Serves 1

3 tbsp natural, sugar-free yoghurt

zest of 1 lemon

2 tbsp your favourite toasted seeds

1 tsp agave syrup

Place all ingredients into a bowl, combine and serve.

Lunch

Courgette and Mackerel Stir-fry

Preparation: 10 minutes, Cooking: 10 minutes, Serves 1

1 tbsp/15ml olive oil
1 small courgette (zucchini), washed and sliced into rounds
freshly ground black pepper
4 cherry tomatoes, halved
100g/¼ cup chickpeas, drained and rinsed
1 garlic clove, chopped or grated or ½ tsp dried or purée
1 small can/¾ cup mackerel in tomato sauce
dash of Tabasco sauce

Heat the oil in a frying pan on a high heat. Add the courgette, grind over the black pepper and cook for a minute or so on each side until starting to soften. Add the tomatoes, chickpeas and garlic and cook for another minute or so until all tender. Turn down the heat, stir in the mackerel and Tabasco and heat through. Take off the heat and serve immediately.

You can stir in some fresh herbs such as basil if you prefer.

Grate over a little Parmesan cheese.

Hot Dressed Salad

Preparation: 10 minutes, Cooking: 10 minutes, Serves 2

2 small Cos lettuces

1 lime

1 tsp olive oil

1 garlic clove, chopped or grated or ½ tsp dried or purée

6 slices lean bacon

freshly ground black pepper

Wash and dry the lettuce, and arrange in a serving dish. Coarsely grate the lime (or use a zester), squeeze the juice from the lime and reserve. Heat the oil in a pan and add the garlic and bacon, frying until bacon is crispy. Discard any excess rind and finely chop the bacon. In a bowl, add the lime juice to the bacon and stir to combine. Pour the bacon mixture over the leaves and toss to coat. Sprinkle with lime zest and pepper; serve immediately.

You could add some grilled sliced chicken breast to the salad.

Chicken, Avocado and Rocket Wrap

Preparation: 10 minutes, Serves 2

1 ready-grilled or roasted skinless chicken breast

1 avocado, peeled, destoned and cut into chunks

1 tbsp mayonnaise

1 tbsp/15ml fresh lemon juice

freshly ground black pepper

handful of rocket, washed and dried

2 stoneground wholemeal tortilla wraps

Cut the chicken into slices on the diagonal and put to one side. Put the avocado, mayonnaise, lemon juice and pepper into a bowl and roughly mash together. Divide the avocado mixture between the two wraps, add some rocket and the chicken. Wrap and serve.

Herby Mussels

Preparation: 5 minutes, Cooking: 15 minutes, Serves 2

2 kg/4.4 lb fresh mussels
500ml/2 cups dry white wine or dry sherry
2 cloves garlic, chopped or grated
handful fresh parsley, chopped
small handful fresh dill, chopped
small handful fresh chives, chopped
chopped herbs to garnish (reserve from above)
60g/4 tbsp olive oil-based spread
2 tbsp Parmesan cheese, grated

Place the mussels and all ingredients (except the Parmesan) into a large saucepan with a lid. Pour over the wine, bring to boil, cover and cook until the shells have opened – approx 10–15 minutes. Discard any mussels that haven't opened. Transfer to a serving dish, sprinkle with Parmesan, garnish with herbs and serve.

Robust 'Root' Soup

Preparation: 10 minutes, Cooking: 10 minutes, Serves 4

1 onion, chopped

2 garlic cloves, chopped or grated or 1 tsp dried or purée

2 tsp olive oil

1 carrot, peeled and chopped

1 sweet potato, peeled and chopped

1 turnip, peeled and chopped

1 parsnip, peeled and chopped

1 tsp ground ginger

half tsp dried chilli flakes

1¼ litres/5 cups organic vegetable stock

Fry onion and garlic in olive oil in a large pan for a few minutes until softened. Add all root veg and cook for about 10 minutes until softened. Add ginger and chilli flakes and cover with vegetable stock. Cook for 10 minutes, blend and serve.

Salmon and Cherry Tomato Frittata

Preparation: 5 minutes, Cooking: 8 minutes, Serves 2

2 tbsp/30ml olive oil

8 spring onions, sliced

1 garlic clove, chopped or grated or half tsp dried or purée

10 cherry tomatoes, halved

4 large free-range eggs

small bunch fresh mint, chopped (optional)

freshly ground black pepper

200-g can/approx 1 cup red salmon, drained, skin and bones
    removed

100g/1 cup frozen peas, defrosted and drained

Heat the oil in a non-stick frying pan and fry the spring
onions and garlic for a few minutes. Add the tomatoes.
Beat the eggs with the mint, season with pepper and swirl
the egg mixture into the pan. Scatter over the flaked
salmon and the peas and cook over a medium heat for
3–4 minutes until almost set. Carefully cook under a
preheated grill for a further 2–3 minutes until lightly
browned on top and cooked through. Serve warm, cut into
wedges.

Rye Bread and Salmon Slices

Preparation: 15 minutes, Serves 2

2 large free-range eggs

2 tsp creamed horseradish

2 slices 100 per cent rye bread

1 little Gem lettuce, washed

2 generous slices smoked salmon

1 tbsp mayonnaise

1 tsp fresh dill, chopped or half a tsp of dried

few sprigs fresh dill to decorate (optional)

freshly ground black pepper

fresh lemon wedges to serve

Boil the eggs until hard boiled, drain and place in cold water. Spread the horseradish on the rye bread and put each slice on a plate. Arrange some of the lettuce leaves on the bread. Lay the slices of salmon over the top. Peel and quarter the cooled hard-boiled eggs, and arrange on top of the salmon. Mix the fresh dill with the mayonnaise and spread over the top. Grind over black pepper to taste. Serve with lemon wedges.

Dinner

Garlic, Lemon and Cumin Pork Chops

Preparation: 10 minutes, Marinade: 2 hours,
Cooking: 15–20 minutes, Serves 4

1 tsp cumin, ground
1 tsp coriander seeds, ground
½ tsp chilli powder
1 onion, roughly chopped
4 tbsp olive oil
juice and rind of half a lemon
4 large pork chops, fat removed
lemon wedges to serve

Place all the ingredients (except the pork and lemon wedges) into a blender and blend into a paste. Transfer into a sturdy freezer bag, add the pork chops and 'squelch' until you are sure all the meat is well covered. Seal the bag, place in a bowl and refrigerate for at least 2 hours. When you're ready to cook – heat the grill to a high heat and grill the chops for 6–10 minutes each side, depending on thickness, until cooked through.

Serve with lemon wedges and low-GL veggies or a crunchy salad.

Great for the BBQ.

Spicy Yoghurt Chicken

Preparation: 10 minutes, Cooking: 15–20 minutes, Serves 4

300ml/1¼ cups natural, sugar-free yoghurt

1 large onion, diced

2 garlic cloves, chopped or grated or 1 tsp dried or purée

1 tsp coriander seeds, crushed

handful fresh mint, chopped or 1tsp dried

1 tbsp cumin seeds, crushed

2 tbsp smoked paprika

zest of one lemon

4 large skinless chicken breasts

lemon wedges to serve

Combine all ingredients, except chicken and lemon wedges, in a bowl and mix well. Place mixture in a sturdy freezer bag. Add the chicken breasts and 'squelch' until all the chicken breasts have a good covering. Seal the bag, place in a bowl and refrigerate for at least 2 hours, up to 24 hours. When you're ready to cook – heat the grill to a high heat. Grill the chicken for 6–10 minutes each side or until cooked through.

Serve with lemon wedges and low-GL veggies or a crispy salad.

Great for kebabs or the BBQ.

Beef Kebabs

Preparation: 30 minutes, Cooking: 20 minutes, Serves 4

2 tbsp/30ml olive oil

2 tbsp/30ml white wine vinegar

4 dashes Tabasco sauce (or other pepper sauce)

1 clove garlic, chopped or grated

700g/1½lb lean steak, cut into cubes

8 firm cherry tomatoes

1 red onion, cut into quarters

3 courgettes (zucchini) cut into chunky rounds

8 button mushrooms

Mix the olive oil, vinegar, Tabasco and garlic together in a bowl. Add the meat, toss to cover and allow to stand for 15 minutes. Thread 8 metal skewers, alternating the meat and veggies. Grill for 20 minutes, turning at least once, until meat is cooked through and vegetables are golden.

Great with salad and houmous.

Sweet Potato and Haddock Fishcakes

Preparation: 30 minutes, Cooking: 7 minutes, Serves 4

4 boneless haddock fillets (or any white fish)
water
4 small sweet potatoes
2 tsp olive oil-based spread
handful fresh parsley, chopped
freshly ground black pepper
2 tsp grainy mustard
2 tbsp/30ml groundnut (peanut) oil

Poach the haddock in a large frying pan with enough water to cover the fish until cooked through. Remove from the water, allow to cool and flake into a large bowl. Boil sweet potatoes until just tender, drain and mash with the spread. Add the flaked haddock to the potato mash. Add parsley, pepper and mustard and combine well. Mould 8 fishcakes from this mixture. Heat the oil in a pan and fry fishcakes over a medium heat on both sides until crisp and golden. Drain well on kitchen paper.

Delicious with salad, tomato salsa and mayonnaise.

Chilli Bean Cassoulet

Preparation: 10 minutes, Cooking: 10 minutes, Serves 6

175g/2 cups lean bacon, chopped
1 tbsp/15ml olive oil
410g/2 generous cups chickpeas, drained and rinsed
150g/1 cup butter beans, drained and rinsed
150g/1 cup sweetcorn, drained and rinsed
400g/4 cups green beans (fresh or frozen), chopped
410g/2 cups kidney beans, drained and rinsed
1 tsp chilli powder
1 tsp paprika (smoked paprika is even better)
3 dashes Worcestershire sauce
2 dashes Tabasco sauce
100g/¼ cup tomato purée
275ml/1⅓ cups organic vegetable or chicken stock

Fry the bacon in the olive oil in a large saucepan until crispy. Add rest of ingredients to the pan, bring to the boil and simmer for about 5 minutes and serve hot.

You can use any combination of beans.

You can use a different meat, or even fish.

Allow to go cold and use as a snack or lunchbox-filler.

Fish Curry with Rice and Beans

Preparation: 15 minutes, Cooking: 40 minutes, Serves 4

For the rice and beans:
200g/1⅓ cups brown rice
2 tbsp/30ml olive oil
1 onion, chopped
2 garlic cloves, chopped or 1 tsp dried or purée
410g/2 generous cups chickpeas, drained and rinsed
zest of 1 lemon

For the curry:
550g/approx 1 lb boneless white fish steaks or fillets
4 tbsp/60ml groundnut (peanut) oil
2.5-cm/1-inch piece fresh ginger, finely diced or 1 tsp dried
2 garlic cloves, finely chopped or 1 tsp dried or purée
4 shallots, peeled and chopped
1 tbsp garam masala (or 2 tsp coriander seeds, 1½ tsp cumin
    seeds, 1 tsp fennel seeds, 3 cloves – ground together and
    mixed with 1 tsp ground cinnamon)
½ tsp hot chilli flakes
freshly ground black pepper
1 tsp turmeric
1 tsp cayenne pepper
410-g can/2 generous cups chopped tomatoes
200ml/⅔ cup organic vegetable stock or water
juice of half a lemon
handful coriander, roughly chopped or 1 tsp dried

Cook the rice as per the packet instructions, drain and set aside. In a large pan, heat the olive oil over a medium heat and fry the onions for 5 minutes. Add the garlic, chickpeas and rice and stir-fry for a couple minutes. Stir in the lemon zest, set aside and keep warm to serve with the curry.

Cut the fish into 5-cm (2-inch) pieces. In a large frying pan, heat the oil over a high heat and fry the fish until no longer opaque. Place fish on kitchen paper on a plate to remove excess oil. Turn the pan down to a medium heat, and add the ginger, garlic and shallots. Fry for 5 minutes, add the garam masala, chilli flakes, black pepper, turmeric and cayenne and cook for a further minute. Add the tomatoes and stock or water, stir and then add the lemon juice. Place the fish carefully back into the pan and cover with the sauce. Sprinkle with a few more chilli flakes and simmer for about 10 minutes. Sprinkle the coriander over the rice and beans and stir through. Arrange the rice and beans on serving plates. Spoon the curry over the rice and beans.

Add a spoonful of natural, sugar-free yoghurt over the curry.

Kashmiri Chicken

Preparation: 10 minutes, Cooking: 35 minutes, Serves 6

60g/4 tbsp olive oil-based spread

2 tbsp/30ml olive oil

3 large onions, finely sliced

10 peppercorns

10 cardamom pods, split

5-cm/2-inch cinnamon stick

5-cm/2-inch piece of fresh ginger, chopped fine or 1 tsp dried

3 garlic cloves, finely chopped or 1 1/2 tsp dried or purée

1 tsp chilli powder

1 tsp paprika

1.5 kg/3.3 lb skinless chicken pieces

250g/1 cup natural, sugar-free yoghurt

Melt the spread and olive oil in a large frying pan with lid. Add the onions, peppercorns, cardamom and cinnamon and fry until the onions are golden. Add the ginger, garlic, chilli powder and paprika and fry for a further 2 minutes, stirring. Add the chicken pieces and fry until starting to brown. Gradually add the yoghurt, stirring constantly. Cover and cook gently until the chicken is cooked through – approximately 30 minutes.

Serve with couscous (with chopped fresh herbs and lemon zest stirred through it).

Serve with one of the marvellous mash recipes – see page 197.

Spicy Indian dishes are surprisingly lovely served with a crunchy iceberg lettuce salad.

Chapter 12

MORE LOW-GL RECIPES – FOOD THAT LOVES YOU BACK!

Now you're getting in to the low-GL groove, here are some more delicious recipes.

We have given symbols to the recipes (see box below) so you can see at a glance how quick they are and if they are suitable for vegetarians.

 Fast and Friendly – 20 minutes or less to make

 Veggie Friendly – suitable for vegetarians

 Foodie Friendly – takes just a little bit more time and effort

---

More Breakfast Ideas

Smoked Salmon and Eggs with Rye Toast

Preparation: 10 minutes, Cooking: 7 minutes, Serves 2

2 large free-range eggs at room temperature

2 slices rye bread

1 tsp olive oil-based spread

2 large slices smoked salmon

1 tsp capers, finely chopped

freshly ground black pepper

1 lemon, cut into wedges

Put the eggs into a small pan of water on the hob, bring to the boil and cook for approximately 7 minutes, until hard boiled. Run under cold water and remove the shell. Toast the rye bread and spread thinly with olive oil-based spread. Drape the smoked salmon over the toast and sprinkle with the chopped capers. Cut the eggs into slices and layer onto the toast. Grind over plenty of black pepper. Serve with lemon wedges on the side.

Sweet 'n' Nutty Toast

Preparation: 5 minutes, Serves 1

1 slice low-GL bread
1 unpeeled apple, coarsely grated
1 pinch cinnamon
1 tsp agave syrup
1 tsp crunchy peanut butter (sugar-free)

Toast the bread. Mix all the ingredients together in a bowl, and spread onto the toast.

Crunchy Nectarine Granola

Preparation: 10 minutes, Serves 1

1 nectarine, destoned and chopped

100g/½ cup natural, sugar-free yoghurt

1 dsp linseeds

1 dsp pumpkin seeds

1 tsp fructose

1 dsp flaked almonds

Place chopped nectarine in the bottom of a glass. Top with yoghurt. Grind linseeds in blender, add pumpkin seeds and grind further. Mix the fructose and flaked almonds into the ground mix. Sprinkle on top of the yoghurt and serve.

Warm Oat and Apple Pot

Preparation: 5 minutes, Cooking: 5 minutes, Serves 1

1 dsp olive or coconut oil

2 tbsp steel-cut porridge oats

1 tbsp sugar-free apple purée (or any other fruit variety)

1 dsp flaked almonds

1 dsp pumpkin seeds

1 dsp ground almonds

1 dsp natural, sugar-free yoghurt

Heat the oil gently in a small saucepan. Add the oats and stir until starting to go golden. Add rest of ingredients and stir until heated through. Put in a pot or bowl. Add yoghurt on top and serve.

One-pot Wonders

One-pot Pork and Orange Casserole

Preparation: 15 minutes, Cooking: 35 minutes, Serves 4

1 tbsp olive oil

1 large onion, chopped

1 clove garlic, crushed or ½ tsp dried/purée

400g/approx 1 lb lean pork loin, cubed

1 tsp ground cumin

300ml/1¼ cups orange juice, with bits

200ml/⅔ cup water

300g/1 medium sweet potato, peeled and diced

250g/2 medium carrots, peeled and chopped

150g/1 small parsnip, peeled and chopped

1 tbsp arrowroot

Heat oil in a large saucepan. Fry onion, garlic and pork for 5 minutes. Add cumin and stir well. Add orange juice and water. Add the vegetables, cover and cook gently for about 30 minutes. Mix the arrowroot with 1–2 tbsp cold water and blend until smooth. Take the casserole off the heat and stir in the arrowroot. Keep on stirring – it should take less than a minute to thicken the sauce. Serve immediately.

Mediterranean Fish Stew

Preparation: 12 minutes, Cooking: 45 minutes, Serves 4–6

2 tbsp/30ml olive oil

2 medium red onions, sliced

3 cloves garlic, crushed or grated

1 can (approx 410g/1½ cups) chopped tomatoes

150ml/approx ½ cup organic vegetable stock

150ml/approx ½ cup dry white wine

1 bay leaf

freshly ground black pepper

750g/1.5 lb firm white fish fillets

1 kg/2.2 lb mussels, cleaned

175g/approx 10 oz prawns (fresh or frozen and thawed)

handful fresh parsley, chopped

Heat the oil in a pan and fry onions until softened. Add the garlic, tomatoes, half the stock, the wine, bay leaf and pepper and simmer for 15 minutes. Cut the fish into 5-cm (2-inch) squares, add to the pan and simmer for 15 minutes. Put the mussels into a large pan with the remaining stock, bring to the boil, cover and cook for 5 minutes until they have opened – discard any that have not. Add the mussels, with their liquid, and the prawns to the main stew, cook for a further couple of minutes or until the prawns are cooked. Turn into a serving dish, sprinkle with parsley and serve immediately.

Grilled Vegetable and Halloumi Pasta

Preparation: 15 minutes, Cooking: 10 minutes, Serves 4

1 large courgette (zucchini), sliced

4 tomatoes, cut into quarters

1 bulb fennel, trimmed and sliced

1 red onion, sliced

1 packet halloumi cheese, cut into cubes

2 tbsp olive oil

2 garlic cloves, crushed or grated

1 tsp thyme (fresh or ½ tsp dried)

1 tsp rosemary (fresh or ½ tsp dried)

300g/approx 6 cups buckwheat pasta

Parmesan cheese, grated

fresh lemon wedges to serve

Turn on grill to a medium heat. Put all chopped veggies and the halloumi into a baking dish. Mix in olive oil, garlic, and herbs and toss all the ingredients well in the dish until well covered. Place under grill until nicely browned on all sides – take out and turn regularly, making sure the veggies and cheese don't burn. Cook the buckwheat pasta in a large saucepan of boiling water until just cooked but still firm to the bite (*al dente*) and drain well. Put the pasta back into the saucepan, add the veggies and halloumi plus any juices and stir well. Serve in individual bowls, sprinkled with Parmesan. Squeeze over lemon wedges for a bit of zing!

Summer Stir-fry

Preparation: 10 minutes, Cooking: 10 minutes, Serves 4

2 tbsp groundnut (peanut) oil

1 red onion, sliced

3 garlic cloves, crushed or grated

1 tbsp fresh ginger, grated or 1 tsp dried

100g/4–6 baby carrots

1 red pepper, sliced

1 yellow pepper, sliced

3 celery sticks, chopped

80g/1 cup cauliflower florets

80g/1 cup broccoli florets

100g/1 cup sugar snap peas or mangetout

50g/1 cup beansprouts

4 tbsp/60ml soy sauce

2 tbsp/30ml dry sherry or dry white wine

freshly ground black pepper

Heat the oil in a wok or large frying pan. Add the onion, garlic and ginger and stir-fry for no more than 30 seconds. Add the carrots, peppers, celery, cauliflower, broccoli, sugar snaps and beansprouts and stir-fry for 3–4 minutes. Add the soy sauce, sherry and pepper and stir, frying for another minute. Serve immediately.

Veggie Gumbo

Preparation: 25 minutes, Cooking: 1 hour, Serves 4

4 tbsp olive oil

1 aubergine (eggplant)

4 shallots, coarsely chopped

4 celery sticks, sliced chunkily

2 tsp smoked paprika (normal paprika will work also)

½ tsp cayenne pepper

3 garlic cloves, crushed or grated

2 tbsp tomato purée

420g/approx 1½ cups chopped tomatoes

1 green pepper, cut into chunks

200g/2 cups okra, thickly sliced (if you can't find okra, add a
    small sweet potato, peeled and cut into chunks and a
    courgette/zucchini, cut into chunks)

250g/½ small butternut squash, peeled and cut into chunks
    (or any squash or pumpkin)

600ml/2½ cups organic vegetable stock

Heat the oil in a large saucepan. Add the aubergine, shallots and celery and cook for 2–3 minutes. Stir in the paprika, cayenne pepper and garlic and cook for a further minute. Add the tomato purée, tomatoes, the rest of the veggies and the stock and stir well. Bring to the boil, and then reduce to a simmer. Cover and cook for 1 hour, stirring occasionally.

Pumpkin Ratatouille

Preparation: 15 minutes, Cooking: 30 minutes, Serves 4

4 tbsp/60ml olive oil

2 onions, chopped

3 garlic cloves, crushed or grated or 1½ tsp dried or purée

1 tsp paprika

½ tsp ground allspice

1 aubergine (eggplant) cut into chunks

250g/approx 3 cups pumpkin, deseeded, peeled and cut into
    chunks

1 red pepper, cut into chunks

1 yellow pepper, cut into chunks

200g/approx 1 cup tomatoes, skinned and chopped (or use
    drained tinned whole tomatoes)

handful fresh parsley (optional)

1 tsp chopped fresh thyme or ½ tsp dried

freshly ground black pepper

Heat the oil in a large pan. Cook the onions in the pan over a medium heat for about 5 minutes until softened. Stir in the garlic, paprika and allspice. Add the aubergine, pumpkin and peppers and cook until they start to soften – about 5 minutes. Stir in the tomatoes, herbs and pepper and cook for a further 15 minutes, stirring occasionally.

Delicious with the Herby Lemon Bulgur Wheat (page 209) as an accompaniment.

Lorraine's Chunky Veggie and Bean Soup

Preparation: 10 minutes, Cooking: 25–30 minutes, Serves 4

1 tbsp/15ml olive oil

1 large onion, chopped

2 cloves garlic, finely diced or crushed

1 medium sweet potato, cubed

1 each yellow, green and red pepper (adds lovely colour as
   well as flavour), cut into cubes or slices

2 celery sticks, sliced

2 carrots, diced or cubed

handful broccoli florets

handful mushrooms, sliced

1 tsp dried crushed chillies

2 tsp grated root ginger

1 410-g tin/2 cups kidney beans, drained and rinsed

1 410-g tin/2 cups chickpeas, drained and rinsed

2 pints/5 cups organic vegetable stock

1 dsp Italian mascarpone cheese/natural yoghurt/crème
   fraîche

freshly ground black pepper

Stir-fry onion and garlic until onions are soft. Add the rest of the vegetables, chillies, root ginger, beans, peas and stock and bring to boil. Simmer until veggies are softish, about 20 minutes. Fill a bowl with the bean soup and add the cheese, stir until the cheese melts through the soup, grind over some black pepper to taste and ENJOY!

Fried Fish with Peppered Oat Crunch Crumb

Preparation: 5 minutes, Cooking time: 6 minutes, Serves 4

handful fine oatmeal
freshly ground black pepper
4 fillets boneless white fish
1 free-range egg, beaten
2 tbsp/30ml organic vegetable or groundnut oil
sprinkling of malt vinegar

Put the oatmeal on a plate, grind over some black pepper and combine. Dip the fish in the beaten egg and coat thoroughly with the oatmeal. Heat the oil in a large heavy frying pan over a moderate–high heat. Fry the fish for about 3 minutes on each side, until cooked through and the oat crumb has turned golden and crispy. Serve with your choice of our recipes for 'healthy' chips, plenty of vinegar and a side salad – mmmmmm, enjoy your guilt-free fish and chips!

Sweet Potato Chips

Preparation: 5 minutes, Cooking: 15 minutes, Serves 4

2 medium sweet potatoes
1 tbsp/15ml olive oil
freshly ground black pepper

Preheat oven to 180°C/350°F/Gas Mark 4. Peel the sweet potatoes and cut into chunky chips. Brush with olive oil and grind over some black pepper. Place on a baking tray and bake for about 15 minutes or until slightly crisp on the outside and tender on the inside.

Great with the Fried Fish with Peppered Oat Crunch Crumb!

Selina's 'Swede' Chips

Preparation: 5 minutes, Cooking: 40 minutes, Serves 4

2 swedes, peeled and cut into chunky chips
1 tbsp/15ml olive oil

Preheat oven to 180°C/350°F/Gas Mark 4. Brush the swede with the oil. Place on a baking tray and bake for about 40 minutes until slightly crisp on the outside but mouth-wateringly soft on the inside.

Great with our healthy fried fish recipe.

Roasted Vegetable Wedges

**Preparation: 10 minutes, Cooking: 30–40 minutes,
Serves 4**

1 small sweet potato, peeled and cut into chunky wedges

1 swede, peeled and cut into wedges

4 new potatoes, washed and cut into wedges

1 carrot, peeled and cut into wedges

1 parsnip, peeled and cut into wedges

1 small beetroot, peeled and cut into wedges

4 tbsp/60ml organic vegetable oil or groundnut oil

Preheat oven to 180°C/350°F/Gas Mark 4. Bring a pan of water to the boil and parboil all the veggies, except the beetroot, for a maximum of 5 minutes. Pick a baking tray large enough to take all the vegetable wedges in a single layer, pour the oil into the tray and put it in the oven until the oil sizzles. Drain the vegetable wedges well, put back in the saucepan, put on the lid and give them a good shake to fluff their outsides a little. Very carefully take the baking tray out of the oven. Put all the veggie wedges into the tray with the oil, turn to coat and put back into the oven for 30–40 minutes or until veggies have turned golden brown.

More Low-GL Dinners!

Olivia's Fabulous Meatballs

Preparation: 10 minutes, Cooking: 30 minutes, Serves 4

1 red onion, roughly chopped
1 onion, roughly chopped
2 cloves garlic, peeled
1 courgette (zucchini), roughly chopped
450g/approx 1 lb lean minced pork
pinch turmeric
1 tsp cumin
1 tsp chili sauce
freshly ground black pepper

Put the onions, garlic and courgette in a food processor and blitz (or grate them all). Place above plus all other ingredients in a bowl and mix all together well. Form into balls and dry-fry in a pan for about 30 minutes, turning regularly.

These go really well with Olivia's Tomato and Roasted Red Pepper Sauce (see page 249).

Vegetable and Noodle Stir-fry

Preparation: 5 minutes, Cooking: 5 minutes,
Serves 4 as a main dish

400g/approx 1 lb buckwheat noodles
3 tbsp/45ml groundnut (peanut) oil
1 large red onion, sliced
120g/approx 1 cup mangetout or sugar snap peas
120g/approx 1 cup beansprouts
1 clove garlic, chopped or grated or ½ tsp dried or purée
2 tbsp/30ml light soy sauce

To serve:
1 tbsp/15ml sesame seed oil or chilli sauce
handful fresh coriander, chopped or 1 tsp dried

Cook the noodles as per the packet instructions until *al dente* or just cooked but not soft, then drain and rinse in cold water until cold and set aside. Heat the oil in a pan and, when very hot, add the onion, mangetout and beansprouts and stir-fry for about 1 minute. Stir in the garlic, then add the noodles and soy sauce and stir-fry together for another minute or so. Take off the heat and serve sprinkled with either sesame oil or chili sauce, depending on your taste. Sprinkle with fresh coriander.

This is lovely with other veggies, too – peppers, courgettes (zucchini) or carrots.

Crustless Spinach Tart

Preparation: 5 minutes, Cooking: 15 minutes, Serves 4

1 large bag (approx 350g) fresh spinach, washed, drained
    (frozen spinach, thawed and drained works as well)

3 tbsp/45ml olive oil

1 medium onion, chopped

2 cloves garlic, chopped or grated or 1 tsp dried or purée

1 tsp fresh thyme or ½ tsp dried

6 free-range eggs

1 tbsp/15g Parmesan cheese, grated

1 tbsp/15g mature Cheddar, grated

½ tsp grated nutmeg (optional)

freshly ground black pepper

Cook the spinach, with just the water left on the leaves after washing, for 6–8 minutes. Drain well in a sieve, pressing down on the spinach to get rid of any excess water. Chop the spinach finely. Put 1 tablespoon of the oil in a frying pan and cook the onion until translucent, stir in the garlic and thyme and add the spinach. Break the eggs into a bowl and stir in the cheeses, nutmeg and pepper. Heat the remaining oil in a medium pan, add the egg mixture and stir lightly until it begins to set. Cook for about 5 minutes until the underneath is set, then invert onto a plate, put a drop more oil in the pan, and slide it back, cooked side up, and cook until totally set.

Alternative fillings:
Sweet potato and red pepper; sweet potato, onion, mushrooms and mixed herbs; herbs and garlic; peppers and bacon.

This is lovely cold for the lunchbox.

Caroline's Fish Pie

Preparation: 15 minutes, Cooking: 20–30 minutes, Serves 2

1 medium cauliflower
1 packet (approx 250g) smoked mackerel
150g/approx 1½ cups prawns (fresh or frozen and defrosted)
juice of half a lemon
freshly ground black pepper
2 tbsp/30ml half-fat crème fraîche
250ml/1 cup milk
2 tsp creamed horseradish
60g/1 cup grated cheese

Preheat oven to 180°C/350°F/Gas Mark 4. Cut the cauliflower into chunks and boil until tender, then set aside in a colander to drain really well. Remove the skin from the smoked mackerel and flake it into an ovenproof dish. Be sure to remove any bones as you do so. Squeeze any excess water out of the prawns, then sprinkle them over the fish. Squeeze over the lemon juice and add the black pepper. In a small saucepan, mix the crème fraîche, the milk and horseradish and gently warm through. Pour over the fish. Mash the cauliflower with half the cheese and spread it over the fish. Sprinkle the rest of the cheese over the top of the cauliflower mash and grind over plenty of black pepper. Cook for about 20–30 minutes until nicely bubbling and browned on top.

Lesley's Albondigas Tonno (Tuna Balls)

Preparation: 10 minutes, Cooking: 10 minutes, Serves 2

225g/1 generous cup flaked tuna or boneless salmon or white
    fish (or a mixture)

1 free-range egg, beaten

100g/¾ cup medium oatmeal

1 tbsp fresh parsley or herb of your choice

1 free-range egg, boiled and finely chopped

1 tbsp grated hard cheese

1 clove garlic, chopped or grated

freshly ground black pepper

extra oatmeal for coating

3 tbsp/45ml olive oil

Mix all ingredients except for olive oil, and extra oatmeal
for coating, together thoroughly. Chill for 20–30 minutes.
Roll into small walnut-sized balls. Roll balls in the remaining oatmeal to coat thoroughly. Heat the olive oil in a pan
over a medium heat and cook, stirring for 10 minutes, until
cooked through and browned.

Serve with a homemade tomato sauce like Olivia's
Tomato and Roasted Red Pepper Sauce (page 249),
Simple Tomato Sauce (page 248) or a low-GL ready-made
one.

Fennel and Ham 'Barleyotto'

Preparation: 10 minutes, Cooking: 30–40 minutes, Serves 4

30g/2 tbsp olive oil-based spread

1 medium onion or 3 shallots, diced

2 large fennel bulbs, sliced thinly

2–3 cloves garlic, chopped or grated

100ml/approx ½ cup dry white wine

200g/1 cup pearl barley

700ml/approx 3 cups organic chicken or vegetable stock

220g/2 cups ham/cooked gammon, cut into chunks

freshly ground black pepper

1 generous handful chopped parsley

fresh Parmesan cheese

Melt the olive oil-based spread in a large pan on a medium heat. Add the onion and fennel and stir gently for about a minute, then add the garlic and cook for a further minute – don't let it burn. Pour in the wine to deglaze the pan, turn up the heat and bring to the boil. Boil for 4–5 minutes, stirring until it reaches the consistency of syrup. Turn down heat and add the barley. Add about one-third of the stock, stirring all the time. Once it is starting to be absorbed, pour in the rest of the stock and cook until it's all absorbed – about 30–40 minutes. Keep an eye on it and stir regularly. When the barley is within 5–10 minutes of being cooked, stir in the ham and grind over plenty of fresh black pepper, stir in well. Take off the heat and stir in the chopped parsley. Shave fresh Parmesan over the top.

Roasts

Roast Turkey

Preparation: 10 minutes, Cooking: 30 minutes, Serves 4

1 large onion, cut into chunks
8 garlic cloves, peeled but left whole
4 skinless turkey breasts
1 tbsp/15ml olive oil
freshly ground black pepper
250ml/1 cup organic chicken or vegetable stock

Preheat oven to 180°C/350°F/Gas Mark 4. Put the onion and garlic into a roasting tray. Rub the turkey breasts with a little olive oil and place on top of the onion and garlic in the tray. Add black pepper and pour in the stock. Cover the tray tightly with foil and roast for 30 minutes or until cooked through.

Roast Chicken Dolcelatte

Preparation: 10 minutes, Cooking: 25 minutes, Serves 4

25g/1 tbsp olive oil-based spread

4 free-range skinless chicken breasts

160g/1 generous cup dolcelatte cheese, or similar

2 handfuls low-GL breadcrumbs (such as Burgen soya and
   linseed)

2 tbsp fresh mint, chopped or 1 tsp dried or purée

Melt the spread in a large frying pan and cook the chicken breasts for 2 minutes. Transfer chicken to the oven and roast for about 20 minutes. Meanwhile, place the cheese in a bowl and mash using a fork. Stir in the breadcrumbs and mint and combine thoroughly. Remove chicken from the oven and spread one side with the cheese mixture. Return to the oven and roast for 5 minutes or until the chicken is thoroughly cooked through. Remove the roast chicken from the oven, slice on the diagonal and serve.

Great with low-GL mash and veggies for Sunday lunch!

Perfect Roast Gammon

Preparation: 20 minutes, Cooking: 3 hours, Serves 6

2 kg (4lb 4oz) lean piece of gammon
water
1 medium carrot, cut into chunks
1 large onion, peeled and quartered
2 bay leaves
1 tbsp/15ml vinegar
1 tbsp/15ml honey
2 tbsp/30g grainy mustard

Place the gammon in a saucepan, cover with clean cold water and bring to the boil. Allow to boil for 1 minute, then rinse the joint and the saucepan thoroughly under the cold tap to remove any excess salt. Cover with clean fresh water and add the carrot, onion, bay leaves, vinegar and honey. Bring to the boil, turn down the heat so that the water is barely simmering and leave to cook for 1 hour 40 minutes. Once cooked, take off the heat and leave to sit for 20–30 minutes in the cooking liquid. Heat the oven to 200°C/400°F/Gas Mark 6. Take the joint out of the saucepan. Spread with the grainy mustard and place on a foil-lined tray. Roast for 20–30 minutes until crispy and browned. Allow to rest for another 20–30 minutes before carving.

■ Serve hot with your favourite low-GL veggies.
■ Serve cold with a crunchy salad or use in wraps.

Nut and Vegetable Loaf

Preparation: 15 minutes, Cooking: 45 minutes, Serves 6

250g/2 cups nuts (walnuts, almonds, pecans, etc), finely
    chopped
175g/5½ cups fresh low-GL breadcrumbs (Burgen sliced soya
    and linseed bread works well)
2 tbsp olive oil-based spread
2 onions, finely chopped
2 cloves garlic, chopped or grated
3 sticks of celery, finely chopped
1 large carrot, finely grated
200g/1 generous cup cream cheese
1 tsp thyme (fresh or dried)
handful fresh parsley, finely chopped
3 large free-range eggs
freshly ground black pepper

Preheat oven to 180°C/350°F/Gas Mark 4. Mix the nuts
and breadcrumbs in a large bowl. Heat the olive oil in pan
over a medium heat and cook the onions until soft. Stir in
the garlic, and then remove from the heat. Put all ingredients into the bowl with the nuts and breadcrumbs and
combine well – easiest to do this with your hands. Pack it
well into a greased loaf tin and bake for 35–40 minutes
until firm. Serve hot or cold.

Marvellous Mashes

Sweet Potato, Cauliflower and Minty Mash

**Preparation: 5 minutes, Cooking: 15 minutes,
Serves 6 as a side dish**

1 small cauliflower, cut into quarters
1 clove garlic, chopped fine or ½ tsp dried or purée
1 large sweet potato, peeled and cut into chunks
30g/2 tbsp olive oil-based spread
large bunch fresh mint, chopped fine or 1 tsp dried or purée
freshly ground black pepper

Put the cauliflower, garlic and sweet potato in a pan, steam or boil until the veg is tender. Drain and put back into the pan. Mash with the spread, then stir in the mint and pepper. Serve immediately.

Great with roasts and cold meats.

Carrot, Swede and Coriander Mash

**Preparation: 5 minutes, Cooking: 15 minutes,
Serves 4 as a side dish**

4 large carrots, chopped into chunks
1 medium swede, peeled and chopped into chunks
1 tsp ground coriander
1 tsp olive oil-based spread

Boil the carrots and swede in a large pan until tender; drain well. Mash with the spread and coriander.

This makes a great topping for cottage pie.

Spicy Mashed Sweet Potato

Preparation: 10 minutes, Cooking: 10 minutes,
Serves 4 as a side dish

4 small sweet potatoes

1 tsp garam masala

freshly ground black pepper

1 fresh red chilli, deseeded and finely chopped (or pinch of hot
    chilli powder or chilli flakes)

1 tbsp olive oil-based spread

Peel and chop the sweet potatoes into chunks, boil until
tender and drain. Stir in all the spices and mash with the
spread.

This can be made in advance and kept covered in a
warm oven – fluff with a fork when ready to serve.

Roasted Garlic and Swede Mash

Preparation: 10 minutes, Cooking: 35 minutes, Serves 2

2 whole bulbs garlic
1 large swede
1 tsp olive oil-based spread
a few sprigs of thyme leaves

Roast the garlic whole on a baking tray in a hot oven for 20 minutes. Squeeze the garlic from the skin and set aside. In the meantime, peel and chop the swede and boil in water for 10 minutes or until softened. Drain and mash with the roast garlic, spread and thyme.

Pea and Mint Mash

Preparation: 5 minutes, Cooking: 5 minutes, Serves 2

200g/2 cups frozen peas or petit pois
1 tbsp crème fraîche
1 handful fresh mint, chopped or 1 tsp dried or purée
1 tbsp/15ml extra virgin olive oil
freshly ground black pepper

Boil the peas until tender. Drain and put into a blender with the crème fraîche, mint and olive oil and blend until fairly smooth. Add pepper to taste and serve.

Mashed Parsnips with Black Pepper and Nutmeg

Preparation: 10 minutes, Cooking: 5 minutes, Serves 4 as a side dish

6 parsnips, peeled and cut into chunks
water
2 tsp olive oil-based spread
½ tsp ground nutmeg
freshly ground black pepper

Cover parsnips with water in a large saucepan and boil for about 5 minutes until just tender. Once cooked, drain really well. Mash with the spread and nutmeg. Add pepper to taste and serve.

Roasted Butternut Squash and Garlic Mash

Preparation: 5 minutes, Cooking: approx 40 minutes, Serves 4 as a side dish

1 large butternut squash
4 cloves garlic, whole and in their skins
1 tsp olive oil-based spread
freshly ground black pepper

Preheat oven to 180°C/350°F/Gas Mark 4. Cut the squash in half and scoop out the seeds. Cut again so it is in 4 pieces. Place on a baking tray. Put a garlic clove on each piece of squash, cover loosely with foil and roast for 20–30 minutes or until tender. After about 20 minutes, remove the garlic cloves from the oven. Allow garlic cloves to cool slightly and then squeeze the pulp out and set aside. Once the squash is tender, take out of the oven and carefully scoop the flesh from the skin. Mash the squash, garlic and spread together. Add pepper to taste.

A Bit on the Side

Sweetcorn Fritters

**Preparation: 5 minutes, Cooking: 5 minutes,
Serves 4 (makes 8 fritters)**

1 large free-range egg, beaten
1 tsp red curry paste
4 spring onions, finely sliced
1 red pepper, deseeded and diced
425g/2 generous cups sweetcorn kernels
2 tsp soy sauce
100g/¾ cup medium oatmeal
1 tbsp/15ml olive oil

Beat the egg and curry paste together. Add onions,
pepper, sweetcorn and soy sauce. Stir in the oatmeal.
Shape into 8 round fritter shapes. Heat oil in a pan and fry
for 2 minutes each side.

Roast Red Onion and Beetroot Wedges

Preparation: 5 minutes, Cooking: 20 minutes, Serves 4

4 small–medium cooked beetroot, cut into wedges
2 large red onions, cut into wedges
1 tbsp/15ml olive oil
2 tbsp/15ml balsamic vinegar or pomegranate juice

Preheat oven to 200°C/400°F/Gas Mark 6. Place beetroot and onions on a baking tray. Cover with olive oil and vinegar or juice. Roast for 20 minutes and serve.

Stir-fried Sprouts

Preparation: 5 minutes, Cooking: 5 minutes, Serves 4

1 tsp olive oil
1 garlic clove, chopped or ½ tsp dried or purée
300g/3 cups Brussels sprouts, sliced
1 tsp olive oil-based spread
30g/2 tbsp flaked almonds
squeeze of fresh lemon juice

Heat oil in a pan and stir-fry the garlic and sprouts for a few minutes until sprouts are cooked through. Add spread and almonds and stir. Add a squeeze of lemon juice and serve.

Onion Bhajis

**Preparation: 10 minutes, Cooking: 10 minutes,
Serves 4 as a side dish/starter**

75g/¾ cup gram (chickpea) flour

2 tsp cumin seeds

1 tsp ground coriander

1 tsp turmeric

½ tsp mixed spice

4 tbsp/60ml water

1 large onion, finely chopped

1 sweet potato, grated

4 tbsp/60ml olive oil

Mix together the gram flour and all spices. Add water to make a smooth batter. Add sliced onions and grated sweet potato and mix well. Heat oil in a heavy-based frying pan and gently drop in spoonfuls of the mixture. Cook until golden brown on all sides. Remove from oil and drain before serving.

Chinese Sugar Snap Peas

Preparation: 5 minutes, Cooking: 5 minutes,
Serves 4 as a side dish

3 tbsp/45ml groundnut (peanut) oil

350g/4 cups sugar snap peas (or mangetout)

4 spring onions, sliced on the slant

2 garlic cloves, chopped or grated

2 tbsp/30ml soy sauce

3 tbsp/45ml organic vegetable stock or water

Heat the oil in a wok or deep frying pan. Add the sugar snaps and stir-fry over a high heat for about 1 minute. Add the spring onions and garlic and stir-fry for another minute. Turn down the heat, and add the soy sauce and stock. Stir well and serve.

Herby Lemon Bulgur Wheat

**Preparation: 5 minutes, Cooking: 15 minutes,
Serves 4 as a side dish**

240g/1½ cups bulgur wheat
zest and juice of 1 lemon
handful fresh coriander
handful fresh parsley
few sprigs of lemon thyme
1 tbsp/15ml extra virgin olive oil

Cook the bulgur wheat as per the packet instructions. Once cooked, drain thoroughly and squeeze out any excess water. Grate the lemon zest finely into the bulgur wheat and squeeze over the lemon juice. Chop the herbs very fine and stir through the bulgur wheat, along with the olive oil. Serve warm or cold.

Green Beans and Basil

**Preparation: 5 minutes, Cooking: 10 minutes,
Serves 4 as a side dish**

15g/1 tbsp pine nuts
1 tbsp/15ml extra virgin olive oil
1 shallot, finely chopped
300g/3 cups French beans
1 tsp lemon juice
handful fresh basil
freshly ground black pepper
fresh Parmesan cheese

Bring a pan of water to the boil for the beans. Toast the pine nuts in a dry pan until golden; set aside. Use the warm pan to heat the oil and gently fry the shallot for a few minutes. Meanwhile, boil the beans for about 5 minutes, until just starting to become tender. Drain well and transfer into a warmed serving bowl. Stir the lemon juice into the cooked shallots. Pour over the beans and toss well. Sprinkle with basil and black pepper, toss again. Shave over some Parmesan and serve.

Andie's Rostis

Preparation: 5 minutes, Cooking: 5 minutes, Serves 1

3 spring onions, finely chopped

1 small sweet potato, grated

1 courgette (zucchini) grated

1 large carrot, grated

1 free-range egg, beaten

2 tbsp gram flour (chickpea flour)

2 tsp olive oil

Mix all ingredients together. Heat olive oil in a pan and fry until golden brown on both sides.

Olivia's Salmon Rosti Topping

Make Andie's Rostis as above. Top each one with a generous strip of smoked salmon and a poached egg. Drizzle a little olive oil over the top, and garnish with some chopped chives.

Sexy Salads

Walnut and Goat's Cheese

Preparation: 6 minutes, Serves 2

1 bag mixed salad leaves
100g/½ cup walnut halves
150g/1 cup goat's cheese, cubed
1 tbsp/15ml balsamic vinegar
1 tbsp/15ml walnut oil
freshly ground black pepper

Wash and dry the salad leaves. Place into a bowl with the
walnuts and goat's cheese. Drizzle over the vinegar and oil,
toss with black pepper and serve immediately.

Melon and Anchovy

Preparation: 10 minutes, Serves 2

1 small melon
small bag salad leaves, washed and dried
4 anchovy fillets
juice of half a lemon
juice of half an orange

Halve the melon and scoop out the seeds. Cut the melon flesh into cubes and put into a serving dish. Add the salad leaves. Drain the anchovy fillets, but keep a tablespoon of the oil. Cut them into slivers and add to the salad. Mix the lemon and orange juice with the anchovy oil and pour over the salad.

Feta and Beetroot

Preparation: 5 minutes, Serves 2

4 whole cooked beetroot, cut into wedges

1 tbsp/15ml walnut oil (can use other nut oils or olive oil)

2 tsp/30ml white wine vinegar

1 tsp grainy mustard

small bag mixed leaves

50g/½ cup feta cheese, crumbled

25g/⅛ cup walnuts, toasted

Combine all ingredients, toss together and serve.

Grilled Pears with Blue Cheese and Watercress

Preparation: 5 minutes, Cooking: 3 minutes, Serves 2

2 conference pears, firm and ripe
80g/½ cup blue cheese, cubed
2 handfuls watercress, washed and drained
freshly ground black pepper

Cut the pears in half and carefully remove the core. Fill the pear halves with the blue cheese, put under a very hot grill for a couple of minutes until cheese melts. Divide the watercress between two plates. Place two pear halves on top of the watercress on each plate. Grind over black pepper and serve immediately.

Chickpea Salad

Preparation: 5 minutes, Serves 4

450-g can/approx 2 generous cups chickpeas, drained and
    rinsed
2 tsp cumin
2 garlic cloves, chopped or 1 tsp dried or purée
juice of 2 lemons
1 red onion, finely chopped
1 tbsp/15ml extra virgin olive oil
pinch cayenne pepper
2 tbsp fresh parsley, chopped
freshly ground black pepper

Combine all ingredients together in a bowl.

Good to make in advance and keep in the fridge
overnight to allow the flavours to infuse.

Watercress Tabbouleh

Preparation: 20 minutes, Cooking: 10 minutes, Serves 4

75g/½ cup bulgur wheat
250g/1 large bag watercress, washed, drained and finely
     chopped
handful fresh mint, finely chopped
juice and zest of 1 lemon
4 tbsp/60ml extra virgin olive oil
3 tomatoes, finely chopped
6 spring onions, finely chopped

Add the bulgur wheat to a pan of boiling water and simmer for 10 minutes. Drain in a sieve and cool with running cold water. Squeeze to remove excess water. In a serving bowl combine the bulgur wheat, watercress and mint. Add all remaining ingredients and mix well.

Allow the flavours to infuse for an hour in the fridge before serving.

Wraps

Sally's Cajun Chicken Wrap

Preparation: 10 minutes, Cooking: 10 minutes, Serves 4

2 skinless, boneless chicken breasts
2 tbsp/30ml olive oil
2 tsp Cajun spice mix
4 tbsp/60ml half-fat crème fraîche
handful fresh chives, chopped
4 wholemeal tortilla wraps
half an iceberg lettuce
8 cherry tomatoes, halved
half a cucumber, sliced

Chop the chicken breasts and fry in the oil on a moderate heat for about 10 minutes until they start to brown. Add the Cajun spice mix and coat the chicken thoroughly. Mix the crème fraîche and the chives in a bowl. Spread each tortilla wrap with the crème fraîche mixture. Place some lettuce, tomatoes and cucumber on each wrap and top with a quarter of the Cajun chicken. Roll the wraps.

Crunchy Veggie Wrap

Preparation: 7 minutes, Serves 1

1 avocado, peeled and destoned
2 sundried tomatoes, chopped
dash of Tabasco or other pepper sauce
squeeze of lemon juice
1 stoneground wholemeal tortilla wrap
handful beansprouts
handful iceberg lettuce, shredded
freshly ground black pepper

Mash the avocado, sundried tomatoes and Tabasco together. Squeeze in a little lemon juice to taste. Place the avocado mash on the tortilla, then the beansprouts and lettuce, and pepper to taste, and roll the wrap.

Goat's Cheese, Sundried Tomato and Rocket Wrap

Preparation: 5 minutes, Serves 1

2 tbsp soft goat's cheese
4 sundried tomatoes, chopped fine
1 stoneground wholemeal tortilla wrap
1 handful rocket, washed and dried

Mash the goat's cheese and tomatoes together. Spread the goat's cheese on the wrap. Add the rocket on top and roll the wrap.

Grilled Veggie Wrap

Preparation: 15–20 minutes, Serves 2

1 courgette (zucchini), sliced

1 red onion, sliced

1 red pepper, sliced

1 tbsp/15ml olive oil

1 tbsp/15ml balsamic vinegar

1 clove garlic, chopped (optional)

freshly ground black pepper

1 small handful pine nuts

1 handful fresh basil or 1 tsp basil

2 tbsp houmous

1 stoneground wholemeal tortilla wrap

Preheat the grill to a high heat. Put the vegetables onto a baking tray in a single layer. Add the olive oil, vinegar and garlic, and toss to ensure all well covered. Grind over black pepper and place under the grill for about 5 minutes or until golden brown, being careful not to burn. Toss, sprinkle with pine nuts and put back under the grill for 2 minutes. Spread the houmous on the wrap, add the veggies and the basil and roll the wrap. Serve immediately.

Prawn Cocktail Wrap

Preparation: 5 minutes, Serves 1

handful cooked frozen prawns (thoroughly defrosted and
    dried)
1 tbsp mayonnaise
1 tsp tomato ketchup
1 tsp paprika
1 handful shredded lettuce
1 stoneground wholemeal wrap

Mix the prawns, mayonnaise, ketchup and paprika together.
Place the lettuce on the wrap. Spread the mixture on top
and roll the wrap.

Snacks and Dips

Dipping Sticks!

The following savoury dips and spreads make great, healthy snacks to keep hunger at bay. Make up your favourite healthy 'dipping sticks' every day so they are always to hand for snacking:

- Carrot sticks (you can also buy ready washed, sweet baby carrots from the supermarkets)
- Cucumber sticks
- Pepper sticks (green, orange, red and yellow – each has its own unique taste!)
- Celery sticks

Halloumi Cheese Slices

Slice the cheese and fry in olive oil, then eat hot or cold as a snack, or add to salads. Use two slices as a snack.

Add herbs and spice for variety.

Seedy Cinnamon Mix

Cooking: 10 minutes

1 handful each of your favourite seeds: pumpkin, sunflower,
flax, linseed, sesame, etc.
1 tsp ground cinnamon

Add seeds to a large dry frying pan with the cinnamon and 'toast' over a high heat until the seeds start to turn golden. Turn down the heat and keep them moving in the pan so they do not burn. Allow to cool and store in an airtight jar.

Both nuts and seeds have a low GL *but* are high in calories, so just a small handful in total of either nuts or seeds (or a mix of both) per day if you are in weight-loss mode.

Choccie Craving Drink

Preparation: 5 minutes, Serves 1

2 heaped tsp cocoa (sugar-free)
2 tsp agave syrup
mug of your choice of milk
sugar-free squirty cream

To sprinkle:
Cocoa (sugar-free) and fructose (mixed half and half in a
    shaker)

Mix the cocoa in the base of a mug with the agave syrup,
add a splash of cold water and blend well until smooth
(you can buy tiny mini-whisks that are great for this). Boil
the milk in a pan and gradually stir it into the cocoa mix in
the mug, mixing thoroughly. Top with squirty cream and
sprinkle with the cocoa-and-fructose mix.

Keep your cocoa-and-fructose mix in a plastic shaker
to shake over the top of your hot chocolate or latte.

Keep a shaker with cinnamon powder and fructose in
too, for a change.

Scrummy Egg Slices

Preparation: 5 minutes, Cooking: 5 minutes, Serves 1

1 free-range egg, boiled
Your choice of the following toppings:
    cream cheese, sprinkled with paprika
    hard cheese slices, topped with a small amount of mayo
      and a slice of tomato
    prawns, cucumber and marie rose sauce
    houmous and celery

Cut the egg into three chunky slices and spread each slice
with your chosen topping.
    A very filling snack!

Egg and Sundried Tomato Pot

Preparation: 5 minutes, Serves 1

1 free-range egg, hard boiled and chopped

1 tsp mayonnaise

1 tsp chopped cucumber

1 tsp sundried tomato

Mix all together in a ramekin.

Baba Ganoush

Preparation: 5 minutes, Cooking: 4 minutes, Serves 4

3 tbsp/45ml extra virgin olive oil
2 aubergines (eggplant), diced
2 garlic cloves, peeled
juice of 1 lemon
4 tbsp fresh basil

Heat the oil in a frying pan and cook the aubergines until soft. Blend aubergines and all other ingredients in a food processor until they form a rough paste.

A great healthy spread or dip.

Avocado Houmous

Preparation: 10 minutes, Serves 4

400-g can/approx 2 cups chickpeas, drained
1 ripe avocado
1 crushed garlic, or ½ tsp garlic powder/purée
juice of 1 lemon
freshly ground black pepper
pinch paprika

Blend the chickpeas, avocado and garlic in a blender. Add lemon juice, black pepper and paprika and mix well.

Nice spread on oatcakes or low-GL toast.

Sardine and Tomato Pot

Preparation: 5 minutes, Serves 2

1 can (approx 120g/1 cup) sardines in tomato sauce
dash Tabasco or other pepper sauce
dash Worcestershire sauce
a few sprigs fresh basil, chopped (optional)

Empty the sardines with sauce into a bowl. Add the Tabasco, Worcester sauce and basil, mash with a fork and mix well.

A good way to eat your oily fish portion at least once a week!

Avocado Snack

Preparation: 5 minutes, Serves 1

half an avocado, peeled and destoned
1 tsp lemon juice
freshly ground black pepper
pinch garlic powder

Mash or blend all ingredients together.

Tuna Snack

Preparation: 5 minutes, Serves 2

1 medium can tuna, drained
half a red onion, chopped
1 dsp balsamic vinegar
1 dsp mayonnaise

Mash or blend all ingredients together.

Houmous Snack

Preparation: 5 minutes, Serves 1

1 tbsp houmous
quarter of a red pepper, chopped
pinch paprika

Combine or blend all together.

Fruity Yog-pots

Preparation: 5 minutes, Serves 1

1 dsp sugar-free fruit purée
1 tbsp natural, sugar-free yoghurt
1 swirl sugar-free squirty cream
Shake of fructose and cocoa (optional)

Spoon the sugar-free fruit purée into a ramekin. Spoon yoghurt on top. Add a swirl of sugar-free squirty cream on top. Sprinkle with cocoa-and-fructose mix from a shaker (optional).

'Sugar-free' fruit purées are a great 'fast-and-friendly' low-GL snack; you can use them in recipes when you need fruit or a bit of natural sweetness. They come in a choice of apple, apple and strawberry, apple and orange, apple and blueberry, apple and apricot, apple and plum or pear, are portable and don't need to be kept refrigerated. See our website for stockists.

Cheesy Avocado Dip

Preparation: 5 minutes, Serves 1

half a ripe avocado, peeled and destoned
1 dsp cream cheese
freshly ground black pepper
squeeze of lemon juice

Mash or blend all ingredients together.

Beanie Dip

Preparation: 5 minutes, Cooking: 5 minutes, Serves 2

1 clove garlic, chopped or ½ tsp dried or purée

1 small red onion, chopped

1 tsp olive oil

half an aubergine (eggplant), chopped

1 tbsp tomato purée

100g/approx ½ cup butter beans, drained

freshly ground black pepper

Sauté garlic and onion in hot oil in a pan until softened. Add aubergine and cook until golden brown. Add tomato purée, butter beans and black pepper and stir-fry for 1 minute. Blend all ingredients together briefly – leave chunky.

Avocado Salsa

Preparation: 5 minutes, Serves 2

1 avocado, peeled, destoned and diced
2 large tomatoes, diced
1 small red onion, finely chopped
handful fresh coriander or ½ tsp dried
juice of 1 lime (or lemon)
freshly ground black pepper

Place all ingredients in a bowl and combine.

Butter Bean and Herb Dip

Preparation: 5 minutes, Serves 4 as a dip

1 can (approx 410g/2 cups) butter beans, drained and rinsed

4 tbsp natural, sugar-free yoghurt

juice of half a lemon

pinch of paprika

pinch of cayenne pepper

1 garlic clove, chopped

2 tbsp/30ml extra virgin olive oil

small handful fresh basil leaves

freshly ground black pepper

Add all ingredients together and blend until smooth. If you prefer it chunky, just pulse lightly until roughly chopped.

Red Pepper Dip

Preparation: 15 minutes, Cooking: 5 minutes, Serves 4

2 tbsp/30ml extra virgin olive oil
1 shallot, sliced
1 clove garlic, chopped
1 red pepper, deseeded and chopped
1 tsp chilli powder

Heat the olive oil in a small pan. Add all the ingredients. Fry for about 5 minutes. Blend all ingredients together until smooth.

Lentil and Bacon Dip

Preparation: 15 minutes, Serves 4 as a dip

1 can/2 cups lentils (approx 410g)

1 tsp Worcestershire sauce

8 rashers lean bacon, grilled and roughly chopped

2 tbsp/30ml extra virgin olive oil

1 tsp white wine vinegar

pinch chilli

freshly ground black pepper

Combine all ingredients and blend until smooth.

Sauces and Dressings

Olive and Anchovy Dressing

Preparation: 5 minutes, Serves 2

large handful pitted green olives
2 anchovy fillets
1 clove garlic, chopped
1 tbsp/15ml lemon juice
1 tbsp/15ml extra virgin olive oil

Place all ingredients in a blender and blend until smooth.
Makes a lovely dressing for grilled or poached fish.

Hot Salsa Dressing

Preparation: 10 minutes, Cooking: 5 minutes, Serves 4

2 tbsp/30ml olive oil

3 tomatoes, chopped into chunks

2 shallots, chopped

1 garlic clove, finely chopped

½ tsp chilli powder

1 tbsp/15ml balsamic vinegar

1 tsp lemon juice

Heat the olive oil in a pan. Add the tomatoes, shallots, garlic and chilli powder and fry for 5 minutes. Take off the heat and stir in the vinegar and lemon juice.

Delicious with fish, grilled meat, or as a warm salad dressing. Also very nice cold.

Garlic and Mustard Dressing

Preparation: 5 minutes, Serves 4

1 tsp mustard of your choice
1 clove garlic, finely chopped or grated
1 tsp lemon juice
3 tbsp/45ml extra virgin olive oil
1 tbsp/15ml white wine vinegar
freshly ground black pepper

Combine all ingredients together in a blender and blend until smooth.

Salsa Verdi

Preparation: 5 minutes, Serves 4

1 tbsp mustard of your choice

1 tsp freshly ground black pepper

2 cloves garlic, chopped

1 shallot, chopped

handful fresh herbs (i.e. tarragon, parsley, chives, coriander or
    dill) or a sprinkling of dried herbs

3 tbsp/45ml white wine vinegar

4 tbsp/60ml extra virgin olive oil

2 free-range eggs, hard boiled

Combine all ingredients and blend, or finely chop eggs
first and then mix all ingredients together well if not using
a blender.

Lovely with poached or grilled fish, hot or cold beef,
and green beans.

French Dressing

Preparation: 7 minutes, Serves 4

1 clove garlic, finely chopped
1 tbsp/15ml lemon juice
2 tsp Dijon mustard
4 tbsp/30ml extra virgin olive oil
freshly ground black pepper

Mix the garlic, lemon juice and mustard in a bowl. Slowly whisk in the oil until creamy. Add black pepper to taste. Blend or shake together in a jar.

Two-minute Fresh Herb Sauce

Preparation: 2 minutes, Cooking: 2 minutes, Serves 2

2 tbsp crème fraîche

1 tsp olive oil-based spread

1 tbsp fresh herbs, finely chopped (choose from parsley,
     coriander, thyme, rosemary, chives)

freshly ground black pepper

Heat the crème fraîche gently in a pan with the spread. Stir
in the herbs and black pepper and serve.

Great with fish or pasta.

Simple Tomato Sauce

Preparation: 5 minutes, Cooking: 10 minutes, Serves 2

2 tbsp/30ml olive oil

3 garlic cloves, crushed or grated

410-g can/2 cups chopped tomatoes

200ml/¾ cup tomato passata (sieved tomatoes – you can buy
in jars or cartons at the supermarket)

1 tsp balsamic vinegar

2 dashes Tabasco sauce (optional)

3 dashes Worcestershire sauce (optional)

handful fresh basil, chopped roughly or 1 tsp dried basil

freshly ground black pepper

Heat the oil in a frying pan, add the garlic and cook gently until soft. Add the chopped tomatoes, passata, vinegar, Tabasco and Worcestershire. Bring to the boil quickly, stirring continuously. When the sauce has thickened, stir in the basil and black pepper before serving.

Great for pasta and all fish and meat dishes.

Olivia's Tomato and Roasted Red Pepper Sauce

Preparation: 15 minutes, Cooking: 15 minutes, Serves 2

1 tbsp/15ml olive oil

1 onion, chopped

1 garlic clove, chopped

1 red pepper, cut into sections, grilled until the skin is black
    and blistered – peeled and sliced

1 410-g can (approx 2 cups) chopped tomatoes

250ml/1 cup water

1 tbsp tomato purée

1 tbsp sundried tomato purée (optional)

pinch fructose

1 tsp cayenne pepper (optional)

freshly ground black pepper

Heat the oil in a pan, add onion and garlic and cook until they are gently softened. Add the red pepper and heat for another minute. Add the rest of the ingredients. Bring to the boil and simmer for approx 10 minutes. Either serve as is or blend for a smoother sauce.

You can change the herbs to use the sauce with different dishes.

Fast Gravy

Preparation: 6 minutes, Cooking: 5 minutes, Serves 2

250ml/1 cup organic vegetable, chicken or beef stock
1 tsp arrowroot

Put 1 tablespoon of the stock in a cup, blend thoroughly with the arrowroot and set aside. Place the rest of the stock in a pan on the hob and start to heat. Pour in arrowroot mixture and stir or whisk until it thickens. Remove the stock from the heat as soon as it has boiled.

If you make sure you buy organic stock it won't contain hydrogenated/trans fats, as many of the non-organic ones do. We like the organic Marigold and Kallo brands.

Sweet Sauces

Orange Custard

Preparation: 10 minutes, Cooking: 6 minutes, Serves 4

600ml/2½ cups your choice of milk

grated zest of 1 orange

8 free-range egg yolks

50g/3 tbsp fructose

1 tsp arrowroot powder

Bring the milk to just below boiling point in a pan with the orange zest, but don't boil. Beat the egg yolks and fructose in a bowl until really light and fluffy – almost mousse-like. Pour the milk over the egg-and-fructose mix, stirring all the time. Rinse and dry the milk pan. Pour the custard mixture back into the pan and place on a low heat. Mix the arrowroot with 1 tablespoon of cold water to make a smooth paste, then stir or whisk into the custard. Take off the heat and stir until it thickens.

To make vanilla custard, replace the orange zest with a teaspoon of good-quality vanilla extract.

Chocolate Drizzle Sauce

Preparation: 2 minutes, Serves 4

2 tbsp sugar-free cocoa
2 tbsp agave syrup

Combine using a mini-hand whisk (these are brilliant) or a blender. Allow to cool.

Use cold for a 'treat' topping for ice cream, yoghurt or porridge.

Apple Compote

Preparation: 5 minutes, Cooking: 10 minutes, Serves 2

2 large apples
2 tsp fructose or agave syrup
1 tsp ground ginger
1 tsp nutmeg
3 tbsp/45ml water

Peel and core the apples and slice into a small saucepan. Add the fructose, ginger and nutmeg and stir. Pour over the water and put on a low–medium heat on the hob, bring to the boil, turn down and cover with a lid. Cook for 10 minutes on a low heat, stirring and making sure it doesn't burn.

Serve hot or cold.

Goes well with yoghurt or added to porridge, or as a topping for vanilla ice cream.

Desserts

Ginger and Kiwi Fruit Salad

**Preparation: 10 minutes (plus an hour to infuse),
Serves 4**

1 medium-sized melon, cut in half and deseeded
2 kiwi fruit (not over-ripe), peeled and thinly sliced
200g/2 cups mixed seedless grapes, cut in half
½ tsp ground ginger or 1 tsp freshly grated ginger
6 tbsp/90ml apple juice (preferably fresh rather than made
    from concentrate)

Cut the melon flesh into cubes, or use a melon baller. Place
in a bowl with the kiwi fruit and grapes. Mix the ginger and
apple juice together. Pour over the fruit and leave in the
fridge for an hour to infuse before serving.

Blackcurrant Brûlée

**Preparation: 5 minutes, Cooking: 10 minutes,
Cooling: 1 hour, Serves 4**

500g/approx 4 cups blackcurrants, washed and stalks
    removed
1 tbsp/15ml water
1 tbsp agave syrup or fructose
150ml/½ cup natural, sugar-free yoghurt

For topping:
20g/1 tbsp fructose
15g/1 tbsp flaked almonds

Put the blackcurrants in a pan with the water and cook
until soft. Add the agave syrup or fructose to taste. Divide
the fruit between 4 heatproof ramekins and put in the
fridge to chill thoroughly. Preheat grill to a moderate
temperature. Spoon the yoghurt on top of the fruit and
sprinkle with the fructose and almonds. Place ramekins
under the grill until the fructose has melted and the
almonds are golden brown. Serve immediately.

■ You can use any other berries.
■ You can use crème fraîche in place of the yoghurt.

Pomegranate Muffins

Preparation: 5 minutes, Cooking: 5–5 minutes (depending on cooking method), Serves 4

30g/2 tbsp olive oil-based spread, melted

2 large free-range eggs

100g/approx 1 generous cup ground almonds

1 tbsp pomegranate seeds

1 tsp baking powder

1 tbsp fructose or agave syrup

1 tbsp/15ml pomegranate juice

If baking in the oven, preheat to 190°C/375°F/Gas Mark 5. Whisk the melted spread and eggs together. Add rest of ingredients and mix all together thoroughly. Spoon a tablespoon of the mix into 4 individual microwaveable ramekin dishes and microwave for about 1 minute each or until springy on top. Alternatively, bake muffins in a moderate oven in a non-stick muffin tin for about 15 minutes. Whichever cooking method you choose, be careful not to overcook – the muffins are ready when light and springy on top.

Pomegranate and ginger go well together, so you might want to add a teaspoon of powdered or grated fresh ginger.

You can adapt and play with this recipe to make other flavoured muffins by taking out the pomegranate seeds and juice and replacing them with:

- a handful of chopped strawberries, raspberries, blueberries, apple, apricot, pear or peach (add a pinch of cinnamon if using apple)
- 50g of 70 per cent plus dark chocolate, broken into small pieces
- 2 teaspoons lemon or orange oil and 1 teaspoon of lemon or orange zest.

Grilled Ginger Pineapple

Preparation: 5 minutes, Cooking: 5–7 minutes, Serves 2

1 small fresh pineapple, peeled and sliced, or a small can of
    slices in natural juice with no added sugar (not in syrup)
1 tsp olive oil spread, melted
½ tsp dried ginger
1 dsp agave syrup
½ tsp ground cinnamon

Arrange slices of pineapple on a foil-lined baking tray and brush with the melted spread. Mix the ginger with the agave syrup and cinnamon and spread over the pineapple slices. Place under a hot grill for 5–7 minutes until golden brown.

Summer Fruit Compote with Greek Yoghurt

Preparation: 20 minutes, Serves 4

400g/approx 4 cups summer berries (fresh or frozen)
1 dsp agave syrup or fructose
4 tbsp Greek yoghurt
handful toasted pine nuts or flaked almonds

Put the berries into a saucepan and gently heat, squashing them with a wooden spoon, for about 5 minutes. Put berries in a bowl, add the agave or fructose, stir together and set aside for about 10 minutes for flavours to combine. Spoon the yoghurt into 4 individual serving dishes. Spoon over the fruit mixture, sprinkle with the nuts and serve.

Baked Rhubarb Crumble

Preparation: 10 minutes, Cooking: 30 minutes, Serves 4

500g/approx 6 cups rhubarb, washed, prepared and cut into
    2-cm/1-inch pieces
1 tbsp agave syrup or fructose
1 tsp fresh ginger, grated or ½ tsp dried
grated zest of 1 orange
juice of 1 orange

For the crumble:
100g/approx 1 cup porridge oats
60g/⅔ cup ground almonds
30g/2 tbsp crushed walnuts
grated zest of 1 lemon
1 dsp fructose
2 tbsp/30g olive oil-based spread
handful flaked almonds for topping

Preheat oven to 180°C/350°F/Gas Mark 4. Pack the rhubarb into a baking dish, drizzle over the agave syrup, stir in ginger and orange zest and pour over the orange juice. For the crumble, combine the oats, almonds, walnuts, lemon zest and fructose in a bowl. Use clean hands to add the spread, making a crumble with your fingertips. Sprinkle the crumble topping over the rhubarb. Sprinkle over the flaked almonds and bake in the oven for up to 30 minutes, checking regularly to make sure the top doesn't burn.

Rhubarb freezes well raw or cooked.

Fruity Cheese Plate

Preparation: 10 minutes, Serves 4

50g (matchbox-sized serving) blue cheese, cut into chunky
    slices

50g Jarlsberg cheese or similar, cut into chunky slices

50g seedless grapes, halved

50g fresh raspberries

1 pear, ripe but firm, cored and cut into wedges

8 sugar-free oatcakes

tbsp olive oil-based spread in a ramekin to spread on
    oatcakes

Arrange all attractively on a large serving plate and help
yourself.

Melting Chocolate Pud

Preparation: 20 minutes, Cooking: 15 minutes, Serves 4

100g/6 tbsp olive oil-based spread

100g/approx 1½ cups dark chocolate (70 per cent cocoa
    plus), broken into pieces

2 free-range eggs

2 free-range egg yolks

60g/3 tbsp fructose

60g/⅔ cup ground almonds

Preheat oven to 170°C/325°F/Gas Mark 3. Grease 4
ramekins or individual pudding moulds. Place the olive oil
spread and the chocolate pieces into a heat-proof bowl.
Place the bowl over a pan of simmering water and allow
chocolate to melt slowly (or carefully melt it for about 1
minute in a microwaveable bowl in the microwave, but take
care it does not burn). Stir and leave to cool. Add eggs
and egg yolks to a bowl. Add fructose and whisk until pale
and thick and mixture leaves a trail on top. Fold in the
chocolate mix and gradually fold in the ground almonds.
Divide into the 4 ramekins and bake for 12 minutes or until
set. Remove from oven and either serve in the ramekins or
run a knife around the edge of the ramekin and turn out to
serve.

Top with sugar-free squirty cream or, for a special treat,
a scoop of vanilla ice cream.

Flapjacks

Preparation: 5 minutes, Cooking: 15 minutes, Serves 8

175g/5 tbsp olive oil-based spread
25g/1 tbsp agave syrup
120g/1 cup fructose
175g/⅔ cup porridge oats
55g/⅔ cup ground almonds
55g/1 cup desiccated coconut (sugar-free)

Preheat oven to 180°C/350°F/Gas Mark 4. Grease a medium-sized square baking tray. Melt olive oil-based spread in a large saucepan with the agave syrup. Stir over a low heat until melted. Remove from heat and stir in fructose, oats, almonds and coconut, and mix well. Turn the mixture into the baking tray and spread evenly. Bake for 15 minutes, remove from oven and carefully cut into squares while still hot. Allow to cool completely before removing from tray with a palette knife.

Baked Apple Custard

**Preparation time: 10 minutes, Cooking time: 30 minutes,
Serves 2**

2 medium free-range eggs

2 tbsp fructose

120g/⅔ cup natural, sugar-free yoghurt

1 tsp arrowroot

1 tsp natural vanilla extract

1 apple, cored and sliced thinly

Preheat oven to 170°C/325°F /Gas Mark 3. Whisk all ingredients except for the apple together until smooth. Divide apple slices into the bases of 2 heat-proof ramekins. Pour custard mix over the top. Bake in oven for 30 minutes or until custard is set and golden on top.

Quick-bake Cinnamon Cakes

Preparation: 5 minutes, Cooking: 15 minutes, Serves 4

1 free-range egg
80g/just 1 cup ground almonds
2 tsp cinnamon
1 tbsp fructose
1 tsp baking powder

Preheat oven to 180°C/350°F/Gas Mark 4. Beat the egg well. Mix all dry ingredients together, making sure you mix the baking powder in well. Fold into the egg. Spoon into paper bun cases or into a muffin tin. Bake for up to15 minutes. Allow to cool before serving.

Alternatives:

To make coconut buns, add 30g of dessicated coconut (sugar-free), or you can replace 30g of the ground almonds with 30g of oatmeal for a different texture. You can also use this basic recipe without the fructose and flavourings to make savoury 'cakes' – try adding grated cheese and mustard or sundried tomatoes!

Chocolate and Almond Torte

This is only for a very special treat or celebration!

Preparation: 15 minutes, Cooking time: 1 hour, Serves 8

250g/1⅓ cups olive oil-based spread
250g/2 cups fructose
250g/4 cups 70 per cent dark chocolate
6 free-range eggs
250g/2½ cups roast almonds, roughly ground

Preheat oven to 190°C/375°F/Gas Mark 5. Beat the fructose and spread together until creamy. Melt the chocolate in a bowl over boiling water, not letting the bowl touch the water, or melt carefully for 20 seconds or so in the microwave taking care it does not burn. Stir the melted chocolate into the fructose. Beat the eggs for about a minute. Fold the beaten eggs into the chocolate-and-fructose mixture. Stir in the roasted almonds. Pour mixture into a 20-cm (8- or 9-inch) pastry ring and bake for up to 1 hour until cooked through.

A–Z OF LOW-GL FOODS

We have included a list of our recommended low-GL foods for extra guidance. The list contains only healthy, low-GL foods (no jam doughnuts or sausage rolls in sight!). We have listed an average portion size, and for tested foods, the GL value. If foods haven't been tested yet, but we assume that they will have a low GL based on similar foods, we have included them (you will see NT, which stands for 'not tested', in the GL column). Foods that contain either no carbohydrate or only a minimal amount we have listed as 0 in the GL column. The 0 foods will have no glycaemic impact and have therefore not been tested.

More foods are being tested for their GL value all the time, including many branded goods. If you would like to keep up to date with newly tested low-GL foods and products, visit our website at www.dietfreedom.co.uk.

You can use the food list along with the recipes in this book to help you keep your daily GL total low. A low daily GL is classed as 80 GL or less and a high GL is 120 GL plus. We have included only low-GL foods on the list: low-GL foods have a GL value of 10 or less per portion.

You can use this as a guide but don't get too hung up on counting (it's boring), just focus on 'swapping' high-GL foods for low-GL foods – it's easy once you get started and will become second nature very quickly. If you want to lose weight rather than just eat healthily, swap to low-GL foods and keep an eye on your portion sizes. You can do this easily by using the 'cupped hands' method of not eating any more at each meal (based on 3 meals a day) than you can fit into your cupped hands.

PLEASE NOTE: If foods are normally eaten cooked, the weights given are cooked weights, unless otherwise stated.

A

	Average portion	GL
Amaranth – 30g popped with milk has been tested as 21 so high-GL		
Anchovies*	120–150g	0
Apple juice	125ml	6
Arrabiata sauce	2–3 tbsp	NT
Artichoke	80g	0
Asparagus	80g	0
Aubergine (eggplant)	80g	0
Avocado	80g	0
Avocado, mint and lime dressing	1 tbsp	NT

B

Baked beans	80g	4
Balti sauce	2–3 tbsp	NT

	Average portion	GL
Banana (green – under-ripe)	60g	3
Banana (yellow and green)	60g	6
Banana (ripe)	60g	7
Bean sprouts	80g	NT
Beef	75–120g	0
Beetroot	80g	4
Black-eyed beans	80g	5
Black pepper sauce	2–3 tbsp	NT
Blackberries	120g	0
Blueberries	120g	0
Bolognese sauce	2–3 tbsp	NT
Bran sticks	30g	NT
Broad beans	80g	5
Broccoli	80g	0
Brown rice	75g	9
Brussels sprouts	80g	0
Buckwheat kasha (boiled)	100g	10
Bulgur wheat (boiled)	100g	8
Butter	20g	0
Butter beans	80g	3

C

Cabbage	80g	0
Caesar dressing	1 tbsp	NT
Carrot juice	125ml	5
Carrots	80g	2
Cashew nuts	50g	3
Cauliflower	80g	0
Caviar	1 tbsp	0

	Average portion	GL
Celeriac	80g	0
Celery	80g	0
Chana dal	80g	2
Chasseur sauce	2–3 tbsp	NT
Cheese – all types	50–75g	0
Cheese and chive dip	1 tbsp	NT
Cheese and onion dip	1 tbsp	NT
Cheese sauce	2–3 tbsp	NT
Cherries	120g	3
Chicken	100–150g	0
Chickpeas	80g	4
Chicory	80g	0
Chilli dressing	1 tbsp	NT
Chocolate – choose chocolate containing at least 70 per cent cocoa. A few squares as a snack is a great healthy choice!	20g (2 squares)	NT
Coffee – be aware that some coffee bar chains add syrups to their coffees which will make them high-GL – ask for plain coffee or a cappuccino.	1 cup	0
Coleslaw	1 tbsp	0
Collard greens	80g	0
Courgettes (zucchini)	80g	0
Couscous	100g	7
Cranberry juice	125ml	8
Cream	1 tbsp	NT
Crème fraîche	2 tbsp	NT
Cucumber	80g	0

	Average portion	GL
D		
Dark Swiss rye bread	30g	9
Diet drinks	1 can/bottle	0
Dried apple	60g	10
Dried apricot	60g	9
Dried cranberries/mango/pineapple/ raspberries/strawberries	60g	NT
Dried prunes	60g	6
Duck	100–150g	0

	Average portion	GL
E		
Eggs	1	0
Endive	80g	0

	Average portion	GL
F		
Falafel	100g	NT
Fettuccine, egg	100g	10
Figs (fresh)	120g	NT
Flax seeds	50g	NT
Forestière sauce	2–3 tbsp	NT
French dressing	1 tbsp	NT
Fructose	10g	2
Fruit tea	unlimited	NT

	Average portion	GL
G		
Game	100–150g	0
Garlic and herb dip	1 tbsp	NT
Goat's milk	125ml	NT
Grapefruit	120g	3

	Average portion	GL
Grapefruit juice	125ml	6
Grapes – black	120g	10
Grapes – green	120g	8
Guacamole	1 tbsp	NT

H

Haricot (navy) beans	80g	6
Hazelnuts	50g	NT
Hemp seeds	50g	NT
Herbal tea	unlimited	NT
Herrings*	120–150g	0
Honey	25g	10
Honey and mustard dressing	1 tbsp	NT
Houmous	100g	<1

I

Ice cream (plain vanilla)	50g	3–8

J

Jalfrezi sauce	2–3 tbsp	NT
Jam (jelly), reduced sugar	30g	5

K

Kale	80g	0
Kidney	75–120g	0
Kidney beans	80g	5
Kippers*	120–150g	0
Kiwis	120g	6
Kohlrabi	80g	0

	Average portion	GL
Korma sauce	2–3 tbsp	NT

L

	Average portion	GL
Lamb	75–120g	0
Leeks	80g	0
Lemons	1	0
Lentils	80g	3
Lettuce (all types)	80g	0
Lima beans	80g	5
Limes	1	0
Linseeds	50g	NT
Liver	75–120g	0

M

	Average portion	GL
Macadamia nuts	50g	NT
Mackerel*	120–150g	0
Madeira sauce	2–3 tbsp	NT
Madras sauce	2–3 tbsp	NT
Mandarins	120g	NT
Mange tout	80g	0
Mangoes	120g	8
Maple syrup	25g	9
Mayonnaise	1 tbsp	NT
Melons	120g	4
Milk, cow's	125ml	2
Muesli	30g	7–16
Mung bean noodles, dried	100g	8
Mung beans	80g	5
Mushroom sauce	2–3 tbsp	NT

	Average portion	GL
Mushrooms	80g	0

N

	Average portion	GL
Napoletana sauce	2–3 tbsp	NT
Nectarines	120g	NT

O

	Average portion	GL
Oat bran (raw)	10g	3
Oat bran and honey bread	30g	7
Oatcakes	30g	8
Okra	80g	0
Olive oil	1 tbsp	0
Olive oil-based spread	20g	0
Olives	80g	0
Onions	80g	0
Orange juice	125ml	5
Oranges	120g	5
Ostrich	100–150g	0

P

	Average portion	GL
Papaya (pawpaw)	120g	9–10
Parsnips (use sparingly)	80g	12
Peaches	120g	5
Peanuts	50g	1
Pearl barley	100g	5
Pears	120g	4
Peas	80g	3
Peas (marrowfat)	80g	4
Peas (split yellow)	80g	3

	Average portion	GL
Pecans	50g	NT
Peppers	80g	0
Pesto sauce	2–3 tbsp	NT
Pilchards*	120–150g	0
Pine nuts	50g	NT
Pineapple juice	125ml	8
Pineapples	120g	7
Pinto beans	80g	5
Pistachio nuts	50g	NT
Plums	120g	5
Pomegranate juice	125ml	NT
Popcorn (plain, microwaved)	20g	8
Pork	75–120g	0
Porridge oats (steel-cut, cooked in water)	30g (dry weight)	9
Potatoes (baby new)	80g	6
Prunes (pitted)	60g	10
Pumpernickel bread	30g	5
Pumpkin	80g	3
Pumpkin seeds	50g	NT
Puttanesca sauce	2–3 tbsp	NT

Q

Quinoa	30g (dry weight)	9
Quorn	100–150g	NT

R

Radicchio	80g	0
Radishes	80g	0
Raspberries	120g	0

	Average portion	GL
Ravioli	100g	8
Red pepper dressing	1 tbsp	NT
Red wine and herb sauces	2–3 tbsp	NT
Rhubarb	120g	0
Rice bran, extruded	30g	3
Rice noodles	100g	10
Roasted vegetable sauces	2–3 tbsp	NT
Runner beans	80g	0
Rye (whole)	30g (dry weight)	8
Rye crackers	30g	10

S

	Average portion	GL
Salmon* (canned or fresh)	120–150g	0
Sardines*	120–150g	0
Sauerkraut	80g	0
Sausages	75–120g	0
Semolina (steamed)	100g	4
Sheep's milk	125ml	NT
Shellfish	120–150g	0
Soba (buckwheat) noodles	100g	NT
Sour cream	1 tbsp	0
Sour cream and chive dip	1 tbsp	NT
Sourdough rye bread	30g	6
Soya (meat alternative)	100–150g	NT
Soya and linseed bread	30g	3
Soya beans	80g	<1
Soya milk	125ml	2
Soya yoghurt	100g	6
Spaghetti, white	100g	10

	Average portion	GL
Spaghetti, wholemeal	100g	9
Spelt hasn't been individually tested so use sparingly for now.		
Spelt multigrain bread	30g	7
Spinach	80g	0
Spinach and ricotta or nutmeg sauce	2–3 tbsp	NT
Spring onions (scallions)	80g	0
Squash (all)	80g	0
Strawberries	120g	1
Sunflower and barley bread	30g	6
Sunflower seeds	50g	NT
Swede	80g	7
Sweet pepper sauce	2–3 tbsp	NT
Sweet potatoes	80g	9
Sweetcorn	80g	9
Swiss chard	80g	0

T

Tabbouleh	50g	NT
Tangerines	120g	NT
Tarragon sauce	2–3 tbsp	NT
Tea (black/green)	unlimited	NT
Tikka masala sauce	2–3 tbsp	NT
Tomato and basil dressing	1 tbsp	NT
Tomato and basil sauce	2–3 tbsp	NT
Tomato and mascarpone sauce	2–3 tbsp	NT
Tomato and roasted onion dressing	1 tbsp	NT
Tomato juice	125ml	2
Tomato salsa	1 tbsp	NT

	Average portion	GL
Tomatoes	80g	0
Tortellini, cheese	100g	6
Tuna*	120–150g	0
Turkey	100–150g	0
Turnips	80g	0
Tzatziki	1 tbsp	NT

U

	Average portion	GL
Ugli fruit	120g	NT

V

	Average portion	GL
Vinaigrette dressing	1 tbsp	NT

W

	Average portion	GL
Walnuts	50g	NT
Watercress	80g	0
Watercress sauce	2–3 tbsp	NT
Watermelon	120g	4
Wheat (whole)	30g (dry weight)	8
White fish	150–200g	0
White wine sauce	2–3 tbsp	NT
Wholegrain bread	30g	7
Wholemeal pitta bread	30g	10
Wholemeal rye bread	30g	8
Wild rice	75g	8

Y

	Average portion	GL
Yams	80g	7
Yoghurt	200g	2–4

	Average portion	GL
Yoghurt and mint dressing	1 tbsp	NT
Yoghurt drinks (sugar-free)	1 standard size	NT

denotes oily fish

FURTHER HELP AND SUPPORT

Our website www.dietfreedom.co.uk is an online resource for all things GL and health related.

You can join our online **Diet Freedom Members' Club** and gain access to the following exclusive services:

'Ask the Dietician'

Personal and confidential responses to your questions direct to your inbox, plus a database of FAQs. We keep our members up to speed on all things GL, including the latest tested foods.

Forums

Our lively forums provide a great support network with members from all over the world. It's fun, friendly and inclusive – we as authors post regularly. It is our inspiration, and the feedback we receive is of huge importance to us.

One-to-Ones

If you need a bit more emotional support with your weight issues, we provide either face-to-face or phone consultations with our team of qualified registered dieticians. Members receive a discount on all services.

Food Lists

Members have access to our *Low-GL-Food List* and portion guide, which is constantly updated with newly tested foods.

	Day 1	Day 2	Day 3	Day 4	Day 5	Day 6	Day 7
Breakfast							
Mid-morning Snack							
Lunch							

	Day 1	Day 2	Day 3	Day 4	Day 5	Day 6	Day 7
Mid-afternoon Snack							
Dinner							

(You can also print this blank plan from our website.)

Recipe Database

We add more recipes each week and are building the largest database of low-GL recipes in the world.

Newsletter

Our fortnightly members' newsletter keeps you up to speed on all things GL, with GL success stories, latest GL research, competitions and offers, and lots of chat.

RECOMMENDED STOCKISTS

Although you can easily follow a low-GL diet without buying special foods, you can visit www.dietfreedom.co.uk for a list of stockists for any of the recommended low-GL alternative ingredients mentioned that may be difficult to find in the high street. For example:

- agave syrup
- buckwheat flour
- buckwheat pasta
- dark chocolate
- gram flour
- oatmeal
- spelt flour

Appendix 4

RECOMMENDED READING

Denby, Nigel, Michelucci, Tina and Pyner, Deborah, *The 7-Day GL Diet* (HarperThorsons Element, 2005)

———, *The GL Diet* (John Blake, 2004)

Denby, Nigel and Baic, Sue, *GL for Dummies* (Wiley, 2006)

———, *Nutrition for Dummies* (Wiley, 2005)

Index

Index of Recipes

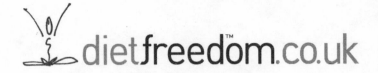
dietfreedom™.co.uk

Online Club

Ask the dietician
Email questions confidentially <u>PLUS</u> searchable database

GL food list
Constantly updated <u>PLUS</u> recommended portions

Forum
Supportive forum, secure, cosy and fun, make loads
of new low GL friends!

Newsletter
Latest GL news, research, tested foods, recipes,
success stories and healthy eating advice

Recipes
Largest collection of low GL recipes, constantly updated

'One to ones'
Face-to-face or phone consultations with registered dietician

www.dietfreedom.co.uk